GROKKING
ALGORITHMS

Simple and Effective Methods to Grokking Deep
Learning and Machine Learning

ERIC SCHMIDT

Table of Contents

Introduction

In the past decade, artificial intelligence has been making waves. From self-driving cars to Siri to Alexa, artificial intelligence is everywhere. But what exactly is it?

The term "artificial intelligence" was coined in 1956 by John McCarthy, a computer scientist at Dartmouth College. His work was based on the idea that computers could be made to exhibit intelligent behavior if they were programmed correctly.

Since then, many people have taken up the mantle of creating intelligent machines—from engineers and computer scientists like Alan Turing and John von Neumann to psychologists like B. F. Skinner and Ivan Pavlov. And today, dozens of different types of artificial intelligence algorithms are being used by companies worldwide: deep learning algorithms, machine learning algorithms... even genetic algorithms!

There are a lot of algorithms out there. Some of them are old, and some of them are new. But if you're reading this book, chances are you've heard something about machine learning, maybe even deep learning.

The world of computer science is a vast and fascinating place. It's also constantly changing, with new techniques emerging every day to help us understand data and make better decisions about how we use it.

One of these techniques is called deep learning. Deep learning allows computers to learn from huge amounts of data, and it's been used to help computers recognize images, understand language, and even drive cars.

This book will teach you all about the Grokking algorithms behind machine learning and deep learning: what they are, how they work, and where they come from. We'll start with the basics of what an algorithm is in general—what it does, how it works—and then move into more specific details about what makes these particular algorithms so powerful.

Grokking Algorithms is a deep dive into the world of machine learning and artificial intelligence. You'll learn what makes these systems tick and how they work.

Chapter 1

Introduction to Deep Learning

Deep learning is one of the most powerful and important tools in artificial intelligence. Its potential lies in automating mundane, time-consuming tasks, freeing up valuable time for more important tasks. That said, it can also be fun, and when you simulate human intelligence, you can learn an awful lot about what it means to be human. It won't be easy to learn, but it is rewarding.

Why This Book?

Do you want to learn about deep learning? Are you interested in artificial intelligence but don't know where to start? Grokking Deep Learning is an excellent choice for anyone who wants to learn about both topics.

Deep learning is a new and powerful tool for the incremental automation of intelligence. In other words, it's a way to program computers to do what they do best: learn from examples and make predictions based on those examples.

Deep learning can generally be described as an approach to machine learning that uses multiple layers of artificial neural networks (ANNs) to process information. A typical ANN consists of several layers (hence "deep"), each containing thousands or millions of processing units called neurons connected in complex patterns. These multilayered networks are trained by feeding them many examples and adjusting their connections until the network reliably produces the correct answer for new inputs it hasn't seen before—a technique known as backpropagation training.

Deep learning is a new and powerful tool for the incremental automation of intelligence. In other words, it's a way to program computers to do what they do best: learn from examples and make predictions based on those examples. Deep learning can generally be described as an approach to machine learning that uses multiple layers of artificial neural networks (ANNs) to process information. A typical ANN consists of several layers (hence "deep"), each containing thousands or millions of processing units called neurons connected in complex patterns. These multilayered networks are trained by feeding them many examples and adjusting their connections until the network reliably produces the correct answer for new inputs it hasn't seen before—a technique known as backpropagation training. Deep learning is machine learning (ML), but not all forms of ML are deep learning. For example, decision trees and linear regression models, which can be very accurate predictors, aren't part of the deep learning family. While predictive accuracy and ease of use are essential measures, deep learning solves complex problems in which data comes from multiple sources (such as images, text, and audio) or when there's a large amount of data available to train on. Deep learning models can also be used to learn new features during training. For example, researchers have used neural networks to "learn" how to recognize cats based only on examples of cat photos.

Deep learning differs from other forms of AI in that it doesn't require much human intervention to tell the computer system what to do or how to perform a task. In addition, it's different from most other types of machine learning because it relies on multiple layers of computing units called neurons that are connected in complex patterns. These multilayered networks are trained by feeding them many examples and adjusting their connections until the network reliably produces the correct answer for new inputs it hasn't seen.

Skilled labor jobs require a long-term investment in education and training (i.e., college degrees). Examples include doctors, lawyers, accountants, and financial analysts. These roles involve higher levels of analysis and problem solving than others; they require a deep understanding of some discipline or field to solve problems. The current trend in these roles is towards deeper specialization within existing disciplines - even as technologies develop new ways of solving problems once considered too difficult for automation (e.g., automated legal discovery).

It is often suggested that deep learning has the potential to automate skilled labor - a trend that will have implications for employment, education, and productivity. However, this claim is not always supported by evidence. For example, while deep learning can automate tasks like image classification (e.g., recognizing objects in pictures), it cannot replace human judgment or decision-making.

This is because humans can make decisions based on multiple factors, while machine learning systems can only learn one thing simultaneously. So, for instance, if you want to build a system that identifies cats in images (i.e., what we call an image classifier), the dataset must contain images of cats labeled as such - not just any picture with felines in it.

In other words, while deep learning has the potential to reduce the need for skilled labor in some fields, it is not clear that this will be an overall trend. Indeed, as automation and artificial intelligence become more common in our lives (from self-driving cars to personal robots), humans may need even more education to adapt quickly enough.

Deep learning is a creative process. You'll learn a lot about being human by trying to simulate intelligence and creativity. You'll learn a lot about being intelligent in making computers think as humans do and vice versa. This process involves both connectionism and symbolic reasoning. And you'll learn how to program complex systems in Python, which will teach you about programming anything in any language—and maybe even about learning languages in general!

You'll also need to know a bit about mathematics and programming, but you can pick up those skills along the way. First, you'll get your hands dirty by implementing real deep learning algorithms in Python—and then you'll turn them loose on real data problems!

Is This Hard to Learn?

If you've ever learned a new programming language or technology, then you know that it's not just about memorizing syntax and functions. Instead, it understands how and why those things work together to solve problems.

Can you learn deep learning in a week? Probably not. Will it take months? Maybe, if you're starting from scratch. But if you have some background in machine learning and are curious about what deep learning can add to your repertoire of tools, then I think the time investment is worth it!

This is simple: Deep learning has numerous applications for improving products across many industries (from natural language processing to image recognition). So, if there's one skill set that every data scientist should be familiar with right now, it's deep learning.

Developing a good intuition for how to solve problems with deep learning can take time. There are many different ways to approach the same problem, and it takes time to learn about all of the tools and techniques available in deep learning. Perhaps most importantly, it takes time to learn about your data - what features might be important and which ones can be ignored? What kinds of preprocessing steps should you take? How should you partition your training/test sets? These questions

are important when building a deep learning model and can be hard to answer. So, my advice is this: If you're starting with no experience in machine learning or deep learning, it might not be the best idea to jump into deep learning without first understanding how traditional machine learning algorithms work. But if you have some background knowledge about these topics (for example, linear regression), then you should go for it!

How Long before You Can Have Some Fun?

You can get started with deep learning (DL) with a simple model and dataset, but there are some important considerations to remember.

> **Start small:** The first step is often the hardest—how do I get started? If you find yourself wondering this question, don't worry! You can take many paths depending on the type of data or problem you want to solve. When starting, it

may be helpful to start with a very simple model that doesn't require much training time or computational power. This will allow for quick experimentation without having too many other variables getting in the way of understanding how everything works together under the hood.

Add complexity gradually: As your skills grow and knowledge expands over time, it's easy for things like more advanced algorithms or complex datasets to feel intimidating at first glance! However, suppose one keeps working at it consistently. In that case, all sorts of things become possible eventually--even really cool stuff like using machine learning algorithms as part of your daily life (for example, by using apps like Google Maps).

Chapter 2

How Do Machines Learn?

Machine learning is one of the most exciting fields in computer science. Artificial intelligence allows computers to learn from data without being explicitly programmed. Machine learning algorithms can be grouped into two distinct categories: supervised and unsupervised. This chapter will look at standard machine learning techniques—from deep learning to parametric vs. nonparametric methods—and how each works.

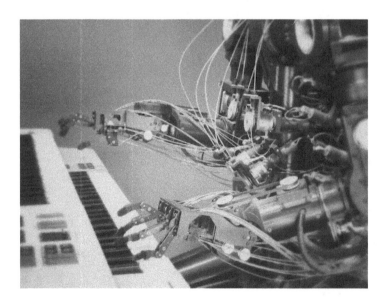

What Is Deep Learning?

Deep learning comes under machine learning, and machine learning comes under artificial intelligence.

Deep learning is also part of the broader category of supervised learning, which requires labeled data to train an algorithm.

Supervised parametric machine-learning algorithms attempt to approximate functions from input variables to output variables. For example, fitting curves or surfaces can do this to data points but often involves more complicated procedures such as neural networks with multiple hidden layers.

Nonparametric methods are more robust because they don't assume any particular form for approximation function. Instead, they use simpler models such as linear regression for most tasks and k-means clustering for unsupervised learning.

Machine learning is the study of algorithms that can learn from data, and it has many applications, including computer vision, natural language processing, and speech recognition. Deep learning is one of the approaches used in machine learning.

What Is Machine Learning?

Machine learning is a way for computers to learn from data.

It is a subset of artificial intelligence, which aims to make computer systems behave in ways generally considered "intelligent," such as reasoning, problem-solving, and learning.

Machine learning can make predictions or decisions based on experience. It builds models from data to learn from experience (the more examples it sees, the better).

Supervised Machine Learning

Supervised machine learning is a type of machine learning where the model is trained using a set of examples.

The most common example of supervised learning is a child learning their ABCs. First, the child will be shown an example (i.e., the letter "A") and then told its name (i.e., "A"). This process repeats with each subsequent letter until all 26 letters have been learned. In this example, we can think about our data as being:

- X -- these are our examples or training set where each row represents one observation or input variable (or feature) for our model.

- Y -- these are known answers for those observations in X that correspond to labels that represent the response variable for each observation (or output variable)

The model is then trained on what we call a dataset which contains the features X and labels Y. This training dataset consists of input data (X) and output data (Y). Next, the model tries to learn how to predict the label for any given input. Then, after we have trained our model on this labeled training data, we will use it to make predictions on new data.

It Can Transform Your Datasets.

Supervised learning is used to predict the value of a variable given the values of other variables. In this way, it can be seen as an extension of linear regression (and all supervised methods).

The difference between supervised learning and linear regression is that the data used for supervised methods contains output labels, whereas linear regression does not. The output labels enable us to train a model to predict new input data.

Unsupervised Machine Learning

Unsupervised learning is a subset of methods for machine learning.

Unsupervised learning groups your data into clusters or similar groups, unlike supervised learning, which uses labels to tell the computer what to do.

Examples of unsupervised learning include clustering algorithms, dimensionality reduction, and outlier detection.

Unsupervised learning transforms datasets without labels, meaning that labels do not have to be used to tell the computer what to do; instead, it can learn from data on its own. This type of machine learning is often used for unsupervised anomaly detection and pattern recognition. An example would be a computer able to identify hand-written numbers without being told.

To summarize, unsupervised learning takes in data from examples and labels it. The computer then uses this labeled information to classify new, unlabeled data. Unsupervised learning is essential to machine learning algorithms because it can help with tasks such as determining how many clusters of similar objects are in a picture or how many different types of customers are buying products.

It Can Group Your Data.

Unsupervised learning is a category of machine learning algorithms that learn from data without being given labels or examples. Unsupervised learning is used to discover patterns and structure in unlabeled data.

Let's say you want to build a classifier to distinguish between fruit and vegetable images. You could train your model by showing it labeled images (for example, apple vs. orange), but what if there aren't any apples or oranges in your dataset? What if adding them would make it too noisy? In this case, you can use unsupervised learning to similar group items based on their appearance and thus create "virtual" apples and oranges!

In other words, clustering is a form of unsupervised learning. It helps you discover patterns in your data that aren't obvious at first glance.

Parametric vs. Nonparametric Learning

Parametric learning is supervised machine learning that uses a parameterized function. Parametric methods are the most commonly used in machine learning, and they vary depending on what happens to the data after it's collected.

Nonparametric methods are less standard than parametric methods, but they allow for better descriptions of a phenomenon by not necessarily assuming it will follow specific patterns. Nonparametric models can capture more complex relationships between variables; however, they can also be more challenging to work with because there aren't any parameters to tune or adjust.

Trial-and-Error vs. Counting and Probability

Machine learning is a branch of artificial intelligence (AI). Generally speaking, machine learning involves teaching an algorithm to learn from data. It's often used in conjunction with supervised, unsupervised, and reinforcement learning methods.

Supervised machine learning aims to predict a label for an unseen sample based on its features by feeding the algorithm labeled training data. For example, a neural network could be trained to recognize objects in images by feeding it thousands of images with labels indicating what object was present in each image. The more training data you provide your algorithm with, the better your model will be at identifying similar images once deployed for use on real-world problems. However, there are limits to how well this works when applied blindly without taking into account any limitations inherent in the problem itself or making informed decisions about what kind of model might work best under specific circumstances (e.g., using smaller datasets when available).

Supervised Parametric Learning

Supervised parametric learning is a type of machine learning that uses a known set of training data to learn a pattern. It's called "supervised" because the system learns from data labeled by a human, who assigns each piece of input data with an output value. The goal is to use this labeled information to make predictions about new inputs—for example, if you're trying to predict whether or not it will rain tomorrow.

If your task is predicting the weather, then you'd need some way for your model to take in various weather factors (say, humidity) and output whether or not it thinks there will be precipitation tomorrow (i.e., rain). The "parametric" part refers to how these parameters are used in this model: The parameters can vary between different examples but still have some relationship with one another; they form your feature space.

For example, in linear regression (supervised parametric learning), you might measure how many hours someone sleeps per night and how much they weigh. Suppose we wanted to predict whether or not someone would be happy. In that case, we could start by determining if sleep has any relationship with happiness - thus creating a relationship between these two variables. That's where our feature space comes from. In this case, the features are "sleep" and "happiness" because they're what allow us to relate these two variables.

Trial-and-Error with Knobs

Let's get back to our example: the neural network. Imagine you're a machine learning researcher, and you have a model that can predict whether someone will be a good customer or not based on their credit card history. You've built this model using your favorite machine learning framework—for the sake of argument, let's say it's TensorFlow (though, for some reason, your non-machine learning colleagues always assume it's MXNet).

Imagine that one day you realize an important factor missing from your model: age! You decide to add age as an input parameter to your neural network and see how it affects performance. The first thing you do is write code like this:

```
def add_input_age(inputs):

inputs['age'] = tf.placeholder(tf.float32,
shape=(1,)).zeros()

return inputs
```

You've defined a function add_input_age() that takes your model's input tensor as an argument. This function adds an age field to the current inputs and returns a new input tensor. Now you need to modify your model's definition so it uses these new input tensors:

```
def define_model(inputs): return
tf.reduce_sum(inputs['amount'],
reduction_indices=[1]) + tf.reduce_sum(input
```

Currently, the model's source code just adds up the values in its inputs tensor's 'amount' and 'balance' fields. You change this to encode age as well:

```
def define_model(inputs): return
tf.reduce_sum(inputs['amount'],
reduction_indices=[1]) +
tf.reduce_sum(inputs['balance'],
reduction_indices=[1]) + inputs['age']
```

As you can see, all you have to do is add a reference to the age field in your input's tensor. Now you have a neural network that takes three parameters (age, amount, and balance) instead of two, and you've encoded age as a factor in your model's output. But what if you decide to remove it?

Your model's code should look like this now:

```
def define_model(inputs): return
tf.reduce_sum(inputs['amount'],
reduction_indices=[1]) +
tf.reduce_sum(inputs['balance'],
reduction_indices=[1]) + inputs['age']
```

You can't just delete the line with inputs['age'] because that would break your model definition. This is because you have defined a model, not written a

program. The difference is that a model defines a relationship between input and output data but doesn't necessarily have to be able to run on any programming language or computer architecture. We're about to show you how TensorFlow makes it easy for you to exclude age from your neural network just by changing the code in your training script.

As you can see, the number of layers in your neural network isn't hard-coded into the model definition. You can change it just by changing a single line of code in your training script:

```
def define_model(inputs): return
tf.reduce_sum(inputs['amount'], reduction
indices=[1]) +
tf.reduce_sum(inputs['balance'],
reduction_indices=[1]) + inputs['age']
```

This is one of the reasons why deep learning is so powerful. It's a simple technique with many applications and can be used to solve problems that would otherwise be extremely hard.

Step 1: Predict

The first step in learning is predicting the next value in a sequence. It's called "predicting" because you're trying to guess what comes next, like you might try to predict which numbers will come up on a slot machine or roulette table.

In this case, we're using a neural network (which I'll explain below) to predict whether a given data represents something red or green. The neural network takes an RGB image as input and produces a probability distribution over different colors (red vs. green) as output.

To train this model, we show our neural network many pairs of images: one image from each pair has been labeled with "green," and the other has been labeled with "red." We then tell our model how accurate its predictions were—did it label every green thing correctly? How about every red thing? This feedback allows us to improve its predictions for new data by changing specific connections between neurons in its hidden layers until the accuracy of its predictions is high enough for us to consider it trained.

It's called "predicting" because you're trying to guess what comes next, like you might try to predict which numbers will come up on a slot machine or roulette table. In this case, we're using a neural network (which I'll explain below) to predict whether a given data represents something red or green. The neural network takes an RGB image as input and produces a probability distribution over different colors (red vs. green) as output. To train this model, we show our neural network many pairs of images: one image from each pair has been labeled with "green," and the other has been labeled with "red." We then tell our model how accurate its predictions were—did it label every green thing correctly? How about every red thing? This feedback allows us to improve its predictions for new data by changing specific connections between neurons in its hidden layers.

So, why do we want to predict in the first place? From a practical standpoint, predicting can help us improve our day-to-day lives. For example, it's what helps your favorite website recommend books to you based on your past activity; it allows self-driving cars to plan routes without getting into accidents. It helps scientists discover new planets and galaxies hidden within vast amounts of data. Yes, predicting is good at making our lives more convenient—and that predicting helps us make sense of the world. For example, imagine that you're meeting your friends at a café you've never been to before. The only information you have is a location in GPS coordinates: latitude, longitude, and altitude (which we'll ignore for now). How are you going to find your friends? You could use predict. Knowing how far away different landmarks are from the cafe can help us predict our friends' future locations.

Step 2: Compare Truth Patterns

Once you have a model, the next step is to compare your prediction to the truth pattern. If the predicted pattern matches the truth pattern, then congratulations! You've successfully learned how to predict this data set and can move on to using your model elsewhere.

If your prediction does not match the truth pattern, then, unfortunately, your learning didn't work this time. This means there was some error in our approach: maybe we had too few samples or not enough training iterations; maybe our network architecture isn't suited for this task; or maybe we don't have enough data points yet (that is, there's no way for us to learn from!). In any case, we must identify what went wrong here so we can try again with different parameters or methods of training until, eventually, our model works well enough!

The learning process would repeat until a model is found that predicts data well enough.

Step 3: Learn the Pattern

In the third step, your machine learning algorithm learns the pattern. This is where it finds out what fits best with the data.

For example, you might look at pictures of animals and want to find out which ones are cats and which aren't. Your machine learning algorithm would try different combinations of features (like "has ears" or "has whiskers") until it found one that told it which animal was a cat and which one wasn't. Then it could tell you if other animals were cats too!

Learning this pattern is the most important step in machine learning. The quality of your learning algorithm depends on how well it can learn from data, and it will often make mistakes or fail unless you give it enough examples.

In machine learning, different algorithms will learn different patterns. So, the best way to find out which algorithm is best for your data is by testing it on lots of examples!

Unsupervised Parametric Learning

A nonparametric algorithm can deal with data of any shape. In contrast, parametric algorithms expect their inputs to be drawn from a specific distribution.

We'll look at the first example of a nonparametric learning algorithm is k-means clustering.

K-means clustering is one of the most common techniques for unsupervised learning and one of the most frequently used clustering algorithms. It's also known as Lloyd's algorithm since it was invented by the mathematician John Lloyd in 1957. K-means clustering works by grouping data points into k clusters, where each cluster is centered around a randomly chosen data point called the centroid. Then, we iteratively update our clusters to reduce the sum of squares within each cluster.

As we can see above, k-means clustering has two main parameters: the number of clusters, k, and the centroid from which to start. These are the only two parameters in our model. Since we have control over the number of clusters and where those centroids are initialized, this is a parametric algorithm. In contrast, kernel density estimation is an example of a nonparametric learning algorithm. Kernel density estimation is another common unsupervised technique for estimating a probability density function. By specifying the bandwidth, we control how much we smooth our data and can make it flexible enough to fit many different distributions. Because of this, kernel density estimation is not a parametric algorithm. Instead, it's an example of nonparametric learning.

Nonparametric Learning

Nonparametric methods use the same algorithm to learn a pattern in the data. They are more flexible than parametric methods since they can handle various problems and data types. Nonparametric models also tend to be less sensitive to noise in the data and thus are more robust than parametric methods.

As a rule of thumb, nonparametric methods work well when the data is complex or high-dimensional. For example, finding a linear relationship between two variables may be difficult if the data set has many features. If we want to find an appropriate model in this case, nonparametric methods can help us.

Nonparametric approaches can also be advantageous in cases where data points' distribution is unknown. In a regression problem, for example, we might want to find an appropriate model even if we do not know the distribution of the predicted values.

Nonparametric methods are also useful when we want to make predictions about future data. These models tend to perform well on new data because they do not rely heavily on assumptions about the underlying process that generated the data.

Counting-Based Methods

Counting-based methods are used in unsupervised learning, which means they don't require any labeled data. So, for example, if you want to group your data into categories or clusters (for example, identifying customers with similar spending habits), you can use counting-based methods as a starting point.

Machine learning is a fascinating topic, but it can also be very confusing. Hopefully, this article has helped you understand some basic concepts behind machine learning. If you want to learn more about this subject, check out our other articles on machine learning!

Chapter 3

Introducing Neural
Prediction via Forward Propagation

Neural networks are a type of machine learning algorithm that can be used to predict the probability of future events. They are inspired by how human brains work, but in practice, they are much simpler than biological brains. As a result, neural networks can be used for tasks like speech recognition, image classification, and more! In this tutorial, we'll introduce neural prediction and show how probability theory provides a convenient language for thinking about neural networks.

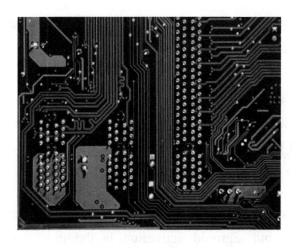

What Is a Neural Network?

Neural networks are comprised of neurons, which are arranged in layers.

Synapses connect neurons, and the neurons within each layer are stacked on top.

The layers have weights (i.e., synapse weightings) that determine how much input from a previous layer is passed along to the next layer. This way, information flows from one neuron to another until it reaches its final destination at the output node(s).

When using a neural network, you'll likely want to specify the number of layers and nodes in each layer (i.e., the topology). Of course, the more layers you have, the more neurons per layer, and your neural network will be more complex. But this also means that it may take longer for your model to train, leading to overfitting. So, a trade-off between model complexity and model accuracy needs to be considered.

The most important thing about neural networks is that they're all about forward Propagation. This is the process of inputting from a previous layer and producing outputs for the next layer in your network. It's also referred to as "the forward pass," It involves calculating activation functions (which determine whether or not a neuron will fire) based on weighted inputs from neurons located in lower layers of your network.

You can use several types of activation functions for forwarding Propagation, but sigmoid activation is the most common. The sigmoid function is a transformation that maps any number to a value between 0 and 1. When you pass in importance to this function, it will return an output value that can be interpreted as the probability of an event occurring.

This transformation is the basis for how neural networks learn. A good example is an image classification algorithm that takes an image as input and outputs a probability distribution over possible classifications. For example, the network may determine that there's a 50% chance your photo contains a cat, 35% of it has a dog, and 15% another animal in the picture.

Next, we'll look at how forward Propagation is used in training a neural network and how the output from this process can be used for predictions.

A neural network is composed of many different types of neurons, each with its unique function. However, all neurons have the same basic structure, including an input and output layer called nodes. A node's inputs are multiplied by weights before being summed together to determine which neurons will fire when you pass in data through your neural network.

Neurons are connected by synaptic connections that transmit signals from one neuron to another. Each connection has its weight, which is adjusted during training based on how much error was made in the previous time step. We'll discuss later what kinds of neurons and connections make up a neural network.

The layers are stacked up, meaning synapses connect them. This is similar to how a human brain works: synapses connect neurons and send signals from one location in your head to another.

If you're a computer scientist, you probably already know that artificial intelligence makes machines more intelligent than humans. But what if we could make computers think like our brains? It sounds crazy, but it turns out that's precisely what some people do.

We need to go back in time to understand how neural networks work. Then, in the future, computers will be able to think like our brains and solve previously impossible problems. The first step towards this goal is creating artificial intelligence programs that can take raw data from real-life situations and turn it into something useful for humans.

To make this possible, we need an algorithm that can take raw data from real-life situations and turn it into something useful for humans. The first step towards this goal is creating artificial intelligence programs that can take raw data from real-life situations and turn it into something useful for humans. The first step towards this goal is creating artificial intelligence programs that can take raw data from real-life situations and turn it into something useful for humans.

Forward Propagation

Forward Propagation is a method for computing the output of a neural network. It takes the values of a neural network's inputs and parameters (weights) and computes its outputs. One might think of it as taking a picture of what you're looking at when you look through your eyeballs, except instead of using your eyes, we use computers!

We start with h_1 (the hidden layer), which has no idea what its input should be; it only knows how many nodes there are in its input based on how many nodes there are in h_{2}'s outputs. So now let's go back to step 2: forward propagating z into every node in h_{1}. This way, each node gets an idea about how much they should affect their weights based on their inputs ($z\)$ and other nodes' inputs ($z^{(i)}$). We then take all these numbers together into one big equation:

```
$$\begin{equation} f(\sum_{i=0}^n
\sum_{j=0}^{m-1}\sum_{k=0}^p z^{(i)}z^{(j)})
= \sum_{i=0}^n \sum_{j=0}^{m-1}\sum_{k=0}^p
W_ij Z_i Z_j + b_n$$\end
```

Forward propagating z through each node in h_{1} then lets us do it again through every node in h_{2}, and so on down the line until we reach our final layer. Notice how we can only go forward one step simultaneously because both layers have the same number of nodes (meaning they're connected). This way, backpropagation becomes just as easy: we take all our inputs, multiply them by their weights, add any bias terms, and get a final value for each node. Then we do it again until we reach our final layer. This process is called forward Propagation.

The basic idea behind backpropagation is that we start with some input, z, and end up with an output, h_{1}. Then we can think of the first step in forward propagating z into each node in h_{1} as multiplying by a weight matrix $W_{\cdot}$.

Neural Networks and Probability Theory

Neural networks are a powerful tool for modeling probability distributions. Let's take a look at how they work.

Consider the following problem: you want to model the probability distribution of an image so that, given an image, you can predict its label. For example, if we have an input image x, then after training our network on many images with known labels, we might be able to accurately predict whether this input is a cat or not. The question then becomes: How do we design our neural network so that it can learn these distributions?

A simple way would be by simply having n inputs representing all possible pixel values in each dimension (for example, $n=256$). Then for each of these n dimensions ($d=1$), we multiply them by some weights (call them $\phi_{d}^{(i)}_j$), which represent how significant each feature value is relative to other feature values. Then sum up all these weighted inputs together and pass through another set of weights (call this $\sigma_{d}^{(i)}_k$)), also called hyperparameters. It determines how much influence each previous layer has on determining this particular output unit's value; finally, we apply an activation function ($g(\cdot)$) on top of all these parameters and obtain the final prediction value!

Probability Density Functions

This section will discuss the concepts of probability density functions (PDFs). PDFs are used to model a random variable and its distribution. They are perhaps the most common way of representing uncertain data in machine learning, so it's worth understanding them better.

A PDF is a function that maps from a set of possible values to the probability of the value occurring. The plot above shows an example PDF for a Bernoulli distribution with 0 or 1 as possible values (we will discuss other distributions later). As you can see, there is no area where both 0 and 1 have large probabilities at once; instead, each value tends to be concentrated around its point along the line axis. This sort of plot is called unimodal because there is only one mode (or peak) on this graph; if there were multiple modes like in many real-world examples, then it would be called multimodal instead!

The goal of probabilistic modeling is usually to predict the underlying distribution of some data. To do this, we must first understand a probability density function and how it works. Probability density functions are used in statistics and machine learning applications such as neural networks; they are a convenient way to represent complex models with many parameters.

The Chain Rule

This is a simple but powerful result. The chain rule for probability densities is the same as for derivatives. This means you can use your knowledge of one to derive the other.

Let's recall that the chain rule for derivatives says:

```
\frac{df}{dx} =
\sum_i\frac{df}{dy_i}\frac{dy_i}{dx}
```

Here, we have an input x and an output y, which is a function of x. We also have some arbitrary function of y, denoted as $f(y)$. This means that the first term on the right-hand side is

```
\frac{df}{dy_i} = df(y_i) = f'(y_i).
```

The derivatives of f are just the partial derivatives of f concerning each of its inputs. So, if we had a function that took in two inputs, like $g(x, y)$, its first derivative would be $\frac{\partial g}{\partial x}$. This is just the usual notation for partial derivatives. Now,

let's consider the chain rule for probability densities. If we have some function $f(x, y)$, then we can write the chain rule for probability densities as follows:

```
\frac{d f}{dx} =
\sum_i\frac{df}{dy_i}\frac{dy_i}{dx}
```

We can see that this is identical to the chain rule for derivatives. The only difference is that we have replaced the partial derivative with a conditional probability of the form $p(y \mid x)$. In other words, we're just conditioning on x when we take the derivative of some arbitrary function f concerning y. The chain rule for probability densities is just a special case of the chain rule for derivatives. The above derivation is useful because it allows us to simply write down what's known as Bayes' Theorem. Before moving on, we should have a quick look at the definition of conditional probability and what it means when x and y are continuous variables.

Using the Forward Algorithm to Compute Normalizing Constants

You can skip this section if you're familiar with the forward algorithm. Otherwise, keep reading!

The normalizing constant of a neural network is the number that enables you to turn its output into probabilities. For example, if your neural network outputs -1/2 for input x = 2 and 1 for input x = 4, its normalizing constant would be 1/2. This normalizing constant does not depend on any specific input—it's a whole property of your neural network.

Normalizing constants are important because they allow us to compare different models in terms of their ability to make predictions rather than just how well they match our data (which will depend on many factors besides their accuracy). For example, imagine we have two models that both compute probability densities: one using hidden units h(x) = tanh(x) and another using hidden units h(x) = sinh(x). Suppose these two models were trained on the same data set but with different learning rates or momentum parameters. In that case, we might think that this makes them equally good at making predictions. But suppose we normalized all their outputs so that they had unit variance (e.g., by dividing each value by its standard deviation). In that case, we'd see clearly that one model was better than the other at producing results close to zero (i.e., predicting no change in values).

Training Neural Networks with the Forward Algorithm

The forward algorithm is a way to train a neural network. It's also the name of an algorithm that computes the output of a neural network. But it isn't just any kind of algorithm; it's important for another reason we'll discuss later in this chapter.

The forward algorithm can be described like this: given a set of weights, compute their output and then backpropagate over those values until you find their gradients (how much they affect error). The result is called "error backpropagation." This process ensures that each weight influences its neighbor as little as possible while maximizing overall accuracy.

The forward algorithm is important because it allows us to train deep neural networks efficiently. Deep Learning is a branch of machine learning where models are trained to perform complex tasks by learning hierarchies of features.

This means that neural networks don't just learn one thing simultaneously. Instead, they learn many different things in parallel, which allows them to solve any problem that can be represented as layers of data (for example, images). And while training happens over multiple iterations, layers are added gradually with each iteration.

Forward Propagation is a step-by-step process that teaches you how to train deep neural networks by taking inputs and outputting predictions. This idea of using forward Propagation with backpropagation has been used for decades since it was first described in 1974 by Seppo Linnainmaa. The input data gets propagated through layers of neurons until an answer emerges at the end. This process repeats over many iterations as more information comes into contact with each neuron.

The idea behind forwarding Propagation is to start with a simple model that can solve your problem but only partially understand the data. Then you will use backpropagation to train it on more advanced tasks like object recognition or speech recognition.

Forward Propagation is a key component of the neural network, and it's essential to understand how this process works. The forward algorithm is an algorithm that solves the problem of learning in a supervised manner by first feeding the inputs into an input layer and then propagating them through hidden layers as neurons process them. This approach has been popularized recently with deep learning technologies like artificial intelligence and machine learning. However, forward algorithms can also be used for unsupervised tasks like clustering or dimensionality.

Probability Theory Provides a Convenient Language for Thinking about Neural Networks, Which Can Be Treated as Computing Probability Density Functions.

If you've ever taken a statistics class or read Richard Feynman's particle physics books, you'll probably have heard of probability theory. Though it can be applied to all sorts of situations—think rolling dice or drawing cards from a deck—probability theory is particularly useful for understanding the behavior of physical systems with many interacting parts. The idea that each part affects what happens next is captured by the notion of an interaction kernel: a function that describes how the state of one part depends on the state(s) and inputs of other parts.

Norbert Wiener first formalized the mathematics behind this concept in his 1938 book Cybernetics: Or Control and Communication in the Animal and Machine (later known as information theory). Paul Webos later applied these ideas to neuroscience in his 1974 paper titled "Backpropagation Through Time". This paper showed how probability density functions could be used to model neural networks. Specifically, he showed how they could be used for gradient descent-based optimization algorithms like backpropagation through time. This led to very good results when trained on certain problems, such as recognizing handwritten digits from MNIST.

Probability density functions are important for understanding how neural networks work. The key idea behind these functions is that each variable in the network affects what happens next through an interaction kernel.

Chapter 4

Introducing Neural Learning
Via Gradient Descent

Neural learning is a particular type of machine learning.

Here are some basic concepts in neural learning:

What Is Neural Learning?

Neural networks are a type of machine learning algorithm. They are inspired by the brain's structure and are used to solve complex problems with large amounts of data.

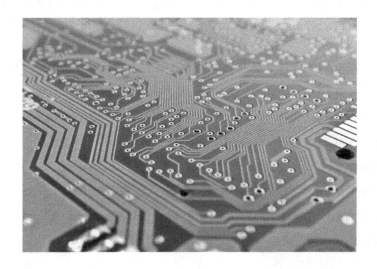

A neural network contains a collection of nodes arranged in layers, with each node sending signals to other nodes within its layer or nodes in different layers. For example, suppose you've taken an Intro to Computer Science course. In that case, you might remember this concept as similar to an AND gate or gate. The output depends on whether all inputs have been satisfied or if any one input has been satisfied.

Gradient Descent

In this section, we'll discuss gradient descent, a method for finding the minimum of a function.

Gradient descent is the process of taking small steps to move towards the solution of a problem. For example, it's often used with optimization problems and can be used to find the minimum value of a function!

The Gradient in Practice

In practice, you are interested in finding the minimum of a function. To do this, you take steps toward the negative gradient.

Gradient descent is one approach to finding the local minima of a function by taking steps in the direction of its negative gradient. The method works by iteratively calculating approximations of the solution at each iteration and moving toward where it thinks that solution lies. Each iteration gets closer to finding an optimal solution because it takes steps in directions determined by some error measure between desired output or result and the actual output or result.

Learning Rate

Learning rate is the size of the step we take along the slope of the error function. This is also known as momentum and can be thought of as a force that helps keep us moving in a positive direction. If the learning rate is too low, we'll lose our way; if it's too large, we'll waste time jumping around trying to find the right spot. Therefore, to ensure smooth progress towards an optimal solution, it's best to start with small values and increase them over time as needed.

Gradient descent is an algorithm that will gradually move in the direction of the steepest decline or negative gradient. In machine learning, we use gradient descent to optimize our models. We refer to parameters as coefficients in Weights in neural networks, Linear Regression, and any other variable that we adapt during training.

One of the most common applications is to fit a linear regression model with a gradient descent algorithm. We start by choosing an initial value for θ (our model's parameters), then update it iteratively while moving in a direction opposite the gradient till convergence.

You can compare your network's predictions to the actual value of each data point by taking the difference between them and then plotting a graph. Then you can see how good or bad the prediction is for each data point.

The median is always better than the mean because it's less influenced by outliers (very high or very low values).

The mode is always better than any other measure because it has all the information in one number and doesn't need any sort of averaging as averages do; it's just as simple as saying, "what is most common?". It also only uses information that appears in some way within all of your data points. This means that if something happens once but never again during training time, then its influence won't affect what happens later on downstream when making predictions based on experience with similar tasks/problems before now."

Why Do We Measure Error?

The most important thing to remember about the error is that it measures how well your model performs. It's a measure of how well your model is learning. And it's also a measure of how well your model is generalizing. So, you want to minimize error because that means you've found the best possible fit for the data and are making accurate predictions based on the information at hand.

You can use several different types of errors, depending on the model you're building and what kind of data you're working with. But generally speaking, all error measures consider both the predicted value(s) and the actual value(s). Your model performs well if your predicted values are close to the actual ones. Let's say we had a neural network that was trying to learn whether or not someone is pregnant based on their age. The

predicted values would be the age of each person, and the actual values would be whether or not that person is pregnant. If our model predicted 0 for someone pregnant, then we'd have an error of

1 (because it missed by one), but if our model predicted 1 for someone pregnant, we'd have an error of 0 (because it was right). The same logic applies to other types of data as well - if your prediction is close to the actual value,

A standard method of measuring error is using so-called "stochastic gradient descent." Stochastic means that you can't control exactly how fast you move towards a particular solution. For example, sometimes you may want to consider moving up one step and down another, but there will be times when you're learning algorithm decides it should move three steps upward and then two steps backward. This kind of randomness is called stochasticity, and with stochastic gradient descent (SGD), we simply take advantage of this fact by measuring our error at each step along the way.

When using SGD, the first thing we do is calculate the slope (or gradient) at each point in our dataset:

$$\frac{d}{dx}j = \frac{\partial y}{\partial x_i}$$

Now that we know this value for every data point in our training set, we can compute its average value across all data points:

$$g^\text{av} = \frac{1}{n}\sum_{i=1}^{n}g^\text{av}(x_i)\tag{4.}$$

This gives us information about how much each dimension contributes overall—it turns out that most dimensions only contribute very little! As such, if we want something like a linear model where each feature contributes equally well, then we can replace each individual g^{av} term with their mean value from $(4.)$.

There are many different ways to measure error. For example, suppose you're using a neural network to predict the number of visitors to a website in the next month. If you predict that there will be 10,000 visits and, in reality, there are only 5,000, then your error is -5%. This means that about 95% of what you predicted correctly was wrong! But maybe it was a good guess? On the other hand, maybe it would have been better if things were worse. These questions depend on what kind of error you care about: the absolute difference between the actual value and your prediction or how far off from reality it is.

Positive Errors Only!

Positive errors are helpful when trying to train a neural network.

Negative errors, on the other hand, are not helpful in the context of neural networks. It's just a mistake during training: it doesn't help and can only confuse other parts of your system that rely on information from this neural network.

Now that you know what neural learning is, we can start to get into the basics of how it works.

The simplest form of neural learning is called linear regression. It's called "linear" because the function has a straight line as its graph and fits a straight line to data points on two variables. It's also called "regression" because it uses all the data points in your dataset to predict which values are likely to occur next (the estimated value). If you haven't worked with linear regression before and want something simple to start with, this might be perfect for you!

Learning Using the Hot and Cold Method.

One way to describe the hot and cold method is as follows:

- The hot direction is the direction of error. In other words, it's where you're currently making mistakes.

- The cold direction is opposite to the hot direction. This means that if something happens in one place, something happens in its opposite place (and vice versa).

The key thing to understand about this method is that it can be used to measure error because it works with information from both directions at once—hot and cold—instead of just one or another at any given time (like with gradient descent).

Backpropagation Is the Core of the Hot and Cold Learning Process

Backpropagation is the core of the hot and cold learning process. It's a gradient descent algorithm that adjusts weights in a neural network based on error scores to minimize those errors.

The first step in backpropagation is determining which direction to adjust each weight: up (more positive) or down (more negative). This direction depends on whether the output was correct or incorrect.

If we were using supervised learning, this would be easy—the correct output would be known and used to inform our decisions about how best to adjust the weight values. But since we're using unsupervised learning here, there isn't an obvious right answer—we don't know what our desired output should be!

It's Called "Hot and Cold" Because the Neural Network Changes Its Weights to Either Move Closer Toward (Hot) Or Farther Away from (Cold) the Expected Output

As mentioned in the last section, neural networks are a collection of weights connecting the nodes. The network learns those weights by adjusting them based on how well it performs on some training data. It does this by adjusting its expectations about how much each weight should influence output for each input and then comparing these expectations to what happened when it ran through all the inputs with known outputs (training set). If it made a mistake, then it adjusts its expectations as if there was some kind of error, which is why we call this process "error backpropagation":

You might have noticed that this process is called "hot and cold learning." This is because the network changes its weights to either move closer toward (hot) or farther away from (cold) the expected output. But why do we call it hot? Let's think of it like this: Imagine if you expected something to happen, but it didn't happen.

Now let's look at a basic example of how hot and cold learning works with three inputs, one hidden layer, and one output.

Now Let's Look at a Basic Example of How Hot and Cold Learning Works with Three Inputs, One Hidden Layer, and One Output

For this example, we'll be using the equation:

```
input 1 * weight 1 + input 2 * weight 2 +
input 3 * weight 3 = activation of hidden
layer 1 + output value.
```

The inputs are set to 0.8, 0.2, and 0.1, respectively, while the weights have values of -0.5, -0.3 and -0.2, respectively (you can set these yourself). This means that our hidden layer will multiply each input by its respective weight (which are all negative numbers). Then add them together to get an intermediate value for that node in our neural network. Next, it is passed through another activation function to produce an overall output result that has been transformed from being based on just three specific inputs into something more complex. Due to interactions between multiple layers within this network, architecture is now being used instead!

The Neural Network Inputs Are 0.8, 0.2, and 0.1

To understand how neural networks learn, you need to know the math behind them. When a neural network learns, it changes its inputs' weights based on what it sees and what happens afterward. The process is simple: each input has weights that multiply the input, and then they get added together and passed through an activation function (like ReLU). The output of this function becomes your prediction!

The Activation Function Multiplies Each Input by Weight to Get an Intermediate Value

In neural learning, you often use the sigmoid function as an activation function:

```
f(x) = (1 + e^(-x))^(1/(1+e^(-x)))
```

The output of the activation function is a weighted sum of inputs to your neural network. After you multiply each input by its weight, add them all up, and then apply your activation function to get an intermediate value.

The Network Adds These Values and Applies Another Activation Function to Get the Output Value. You Can Think of This as a Confidence Value or Probability That This Result Is the Right One

The network adds these values and applies another activation function to get the output value. You can think of this as a confidence value or probability that this result is the right one.

The final layer of the neural network is called the output layer, which contains several nodes that will define your model's outputs. The number of nodes in this layer depends on how many different outputs you want to predict. For example, if you are building a machine learning model for image classification, then there may be an input image (e.g., a picture) and two outputs: "dog" or "cat". In this case, there would be two nodes in the final layer—one representing each word (or label).

For Simplicity, Let's Say You Want Your Desired Output to Be 0.01, so You Know This Result Is Wrong. You Compare Your Result to Your Expected Output and Find Out Your Network Made a Huge Error!

The error score is the difference between the actual output and your desired output. For example, if you wanted your network to predict 0.01, but it predicted 0.98 instead, you would have an error score of -0.98. The neural network is trying to learn how to predict the output based on the input using this error score as feedback, so it can adjust its internal weights accordingly.

This Might Have Happened Because the Weights Are Set Incorrectly, So You'll Use Backpropagation to Adjust Them Based on Your Error Score

The core of the hot and cold learning process is backpropagation. Backpropagation is an algorithm that adjusts the network's weights based on your error score. The error score simply measures how far off your network's output was from what you expected it to be. If, for example, I told you that a dog was a cat, you'd probably expect to see whiskers (a cat's defining feature) and fur (another characteristic). If instead, I showed you a dog without either of those traits, then your error score would be high—you were very surprised by this outcome!

To correct this situation, backpropagation trains the neural network with information about how much better or worse its performance has been compared to its desired outcome in each training example.

These adjustments are made over time through many iterations until your model eventually reaches an acceptable level of accuracy on new samples that it hasn't seen before.

In This Case, You'll Use Gradient Descent, in Which Backpropagation Will Subtract a Small Portion of Your Error Score from the Original Weight for Each Node to Adjust It Downward

In this case, you'll use gradient descent, in which backpropagation will subtract a small portion of your error score from the original weight for each node to adjust it downward. This can be visualized as a ball rolling down a hill and then bouncing off an obstacle. You'll notice that once you get below the obstacle, there's no longer any reason for your ball to continue moving downward—so it bounces back up toward its starting point.

In neural networks trained with gradient descent, we're trying to find the best possible configuration of weights given our training dataset (much like how we want our ball to reach its lowest point).

Hot and Cold Characteristics

Hot learning is fast, efficient, and easy to implement but doesn't scale well. Cold learning is the opposite: slow, inefficient, and difficult to implement. However, it can be scaled up easily.

Which one is better? It depends on what you are trying to achieve and how much money you have.

It's Not Efficient.

Neural networks are a popular tool for solving complex problems, but they still have limitations. The most notable of these is that they're hard to train properly. Here are some common problems that cause neural networks to fail:

It's hard to predict what you want to predict. Neural networks are created by feeding thousands or millions of examples into the network, so it can find patterns in them and adjust their weights accordingly. But what if you don't give enough examples? Or what if you give it too many? Then the network may not be able to learn well enough from those few training cases and will end up with inaccurate predictions on new data points.

It's hard to measure error. How do you know which performs best when trying out different models and algorithms? You could compare each model against an existing benchmark (like time-series data). Still, there may be other benchmarks that better represent your situation. In addition, performance metrics differ depending on whether we're looking at classification accuracy versus precision/recall metrics or something else altogether! In this case, we need more flexible methodologies which allow flexibility within our evaluation framework and adaptability when presented with new challenges, such as incomplete datasets without historical patterns available beforehand.

You Can't Always Produce the Goal Prediction You Expect.

This can happen for several reasons:

- You don't know the right answer (e.g., optimizing a sales conversion rate that depends on many factors).

- You don't know how to measure success (e.g., achieving a certain profit level).

- You don't know how to measure error (e.g., estimating how far away from an optimal value you are or predicting whether or not someone will buy something).

Using Error to Calculate Direction and Amount

To train the network, you need to calculate the direction and the amount of change. This can be done by calculating the "gradient" of your error function. The gradient is the vector that points toward the greatest increase (or decrease) in your cost function value at any given point. To calculate it, you first need to compute your derivative concerning each weight in your neural network:

You then add all these derivatives from each weight and divide them by their respective learning rates. This gives you an estimate of how much learning should happen for each weight when you update its value using gradient descent or another optimization method such as stochastic gradient descent (SGD). These updated values are then used as inputs into another iteration of forwarding propagation. Finally, they get multiplied by their corresponding bias term before being added together with all other activations for us once again to obtain our final output prediction!

Let's look at one iteration of gradient descent, starting with the weights' set and initial values.

The first thing that happens is that we calculate the error. The error is the difference between our guess (the output from our neural network) and what we want it to be (the correct answer). If you're trying to predict whether someone will survive cancer, for example, then your neural network's guess would be some number between 0 and 100%. A high number means a good chance they'll survive; conversely, a low number means an even better chance they won't survive.

We then calculate this value by comparing each input value in turn with its corresponding output value after being processed by the neurons in your neural network:

Once we've done that, we calculate the gradient. The gradient is how our error changes as the value of a single weight changes. So, in other words, if you change a weight's value and your error gets smaller, then you know that changing this particular weight's value positively affects your overall error.

When you're starting with neural networks, it can be hard to wrap your head around the idea that learning is just about reducing error.

Thinking of a neural network as a system for finding weights that minimize error can help you understand why the whole process works.

Before we go over how gradient descent does this, let's take a quick detour into what "error" means in machine learning.

A learning rate can modify the weight to reduce the error. Here's how it works:

You start with a random weight and make small adjustments until you reach a point where your error is as small as possible.

Now go forth and reduce your error!

Example with Code

Let's take a look at the code. First, we import the data from our file into Python. Next, we create three functions:

1. difference_calculate()

2. direction_calculate()

3. amount_calculate()

The first of these will calculate the difference between two points on your dataset. The second will give you an angle between those two points (in degrees). And finally, amount_calculate() provides information about how far apart those two points are in units of distance (in this case meters).

Let's test it out!

```
import numpy as np import matplotlib.pyplot
as plt from scipy import io %matplotlib
inline def difference_calculate(x1, y1, x2,
```

```python
y2): diff = np.array([x2 - x1, y2 - y1])
return diff def direction_calculate(diff):
direction = np.arctan2(diff[0],

diff[1])*(180/np.pi) return direction def
amount_calculate(x1, y1, x2, y2): amount =
np.sqrt((x2 - x1)**2 + (y2 - y1)**2) return
amount def error_calculate(total_error):
error = total_error / len(total_error) * 100

return error def error_direction(angle1,
angle2): error = (angle1 - angle2) / np.pi *
180 return error

difference_calculate(0, 0, 5, 5)
direction_calculate(np.array([5, 5]))
amount_calculate(0, 0, 5, 5)
error_calculate(np.array([5., 5.]))
error_direction(5., 45.)
```

Another Example with Code

In this example, you will calculate the direction and amount of a change in price for a stock. Because there is no way to know whether the price will go up or down (this is called a discrete random variable), we'll use an indicator variable to indicate if the price has changed. We'll call this indicator variable "change" and set it equal to 1 if there was an increase in price, 0 if there was no change in price, or -1 if there was a decrease in price:

```python
```python if price_today > price_yesterday:
change = 1 elif price_today ==
price_yesterday: change = 0 else: #price
today
```
```

```
change = -1 print("There was a " +
str(change) + " point change in price.")  ```
```

Now we can move on to the actual error calculation. We first need a variable called "target" that will represent our desired price. We'll set this variable equal to 100, which means we want the price of our stock to be 100:

```python
target = 100
```

Next, we'll create a new variable named "error."

We can then print 'error' to the screen. If the current price of our stock is 100, then we will see 'error' equal to zero:

```python
#
```

If current price is 100, print 0 if change == 1:

```
error = target - (price_today + change) elif
change == 0: error = target - price_today
else: #change == -1 error = target -
(price_today + change) print(error)
```

That's great, but what if the current price of our stock is something other than 100? Let's say it's 90. In that case, we would see an error of 10:

```python
#
```

If current price is 90, print 10 if change == 1:

```
error = target - (price_today + change) elif
change == 0: error = target - price_today
```

```
else: #change == -1 error = target -
(price_today + change) print(error)
```

Now let's say our stock price is 110. In that case, we would see an error of -10:

```python #
```

If current price is 110, print -10 if change == 1:

```
error = target - (price_today + change) elif
change == 0: error = target - price_today
else: #change == -1 error = target -
(price_today +change) print(error)
```

Now, let's say our stock price is 50, and we want to be closer to 100. We could buy a stock on Monday, wait until Tuesday, and then sell it on Wednesday. However, that would take three days and cost us money in transaction fees. Another option is to buy a stock on Monday and sell it the next day instead of waiting until the following day.

The direction and amount of error is determined by the goal we set at the beginning of our learning process. If our goal was to get closer to 100 (as in this example), then we would see a positive error when our stock price was less than 100 and a negative error when it was greater than 100.

What Is a Function? How Do You Understand One?

Let's say you're trying to figure out how much money you'll have if you save $100 per month for 10 years. To solve this problem, we can consider the amount of money in your account as f(t), where t is time, and f is a function. We want to find the value of f at t=10, so let's pick an arbitrary value in our interval (say 0). Then we need to find which values of t give us 0 dollars after 10 years. That gives us two points on our graph: (0, 0) and (10, ?).

We can calculate these ratios easily:

```
f'(0) = 100/(1-0)^10 = 100/0 = 100
```

Now we can use this as our slope and draw a linear function through (0, 0) with slope 100. Since the slope of a line is the same for any horizontal line through it, we can then draw lines parallel to this through all other points in our interval. From there, we can find out which values of t give us zero dollars after 10 years. That's how you solve a simple equation like y=x+2; you take a point on either side of zero and calculate the slope. With more complicated equations, finding points whose slopes are easy to calculate is important. For example, if

```
f(t)=5t^2-3t+10, then f'(0) = 0 and f'(1) =
8.
```

These aren't very helpful slopes to have! So we need to find points that make the slope easier to calculate. We can try

```
f'(x)=5(x^2-3x+10),
```

and we can use algebra to find the zeroes of this function. The zeroes are

```
x=0, 1, 2.
```

But when you plug in 0 for x, you get

```
f' (0)=50-30+10=30.
```

When you plug in 1 for x, you get

```
f' (1)=50-3+10=57.
```

Finally, when you plug in 2 for x, you get

```
f' (2)=50-6+10
```

These three points all have slopes that are easy to calculate, so they give us a place to start. We can use this as our slope and draw a linear function through (0, 0) with slope 100. Since the slope of a line is the same for any horizontal line through it, we can then draw lines parallel to this through all other points in our interval. From there, we can find out which values of t give us zero dollars after 10 years.

Tunnel Vision

In neural learning, there is a common problem called "tunnel vision."

This happens when you're trying to learn something new and get stuck on one concept.

For example, if you are training a neural network to recognize cats in images, but all your training data has been photos of tabby cats (striped cats), then the network will be able to do that well! But it won't know how to recognize other types of cats at all. This is because the concept of "tabby" has been embedded in too many layers within its architecture.

You can see this effect in humans, too: if someone only ever sees horses with long manes and tails, they might think that's what all horses look like! The same goes for dogs that only have fur on their heads: they think every dog has hair just like them (and therefore don't understand how any other dog could exist).

Example

This example is a simple neural network that can learn to recognize handwritten numbers.

The input layer has 10 neurons, one for each row and column of pixels in the image. The output layer has 1 neuron for each possible number (1-10) that the model could recognize.

The best way to learn about neural networks is by playing with them yourself. To get started, you can use the following starter code:

```
import numpy as np from keras.datasets
import mnist from keras.utils import
to_categorical from sklearn.neural_network
import MLPClassifier data =
mnist.load_data() (X, y), (X_test, y_test) =
data

print(X.shape) # Add the channel dimension
for color images data = data.reshape((-1,
28, 28, 1)) print(data.shape) data_labels =
to_categorical(y) model =
```

```
MLPClassifier(hidden_layer_sizes=(64, 64),
activation='relu') model.fit(X.reshape(-1,
784), data_labels)
```

Congratulations! You've just trained your first neural network.

Introducing Derivatives

One of the most important concepts in mathematics is the derivative. Unfortunately, it's also pretty much impossible to understand unless you have a solid understanding of calculus, but it can be explained in simpler terms.

The derivative is the rate of change between two variables. In other words, it's how much one variable changes when another varies. The simplest example is probably that of an equation:

```
y = mx + b
```

If we introduce another variable (x), we can write this as:

```
y' = m * x + b * (1 - y)
```

This tells us that if we increase y by 1 over time, y' will increase by $1/m$ times x. Similarly, if we decrease y by 1 over some time and keep everything else constant, y' will decrease by $1/(m+1)$ times x (because there are more places to go).

Using Derivatives to Learn

A derivative tells you the rate of change concerning another quantity. It's a key concept in calculus, and it allows us to find the optimal value for something by making small adjustments over time. For example, if you want to minimize the error on an equation like x = sin(x), then you need to know how fast the sine function changes as we move along the x-axis. The derivative lets us calculate this change. We can then use this information (in conjunction with other variables) to make tiny adjustments that eventually lead us straight toward zero error!

This might sound complicated but don't worry—it's pretty simple once you understand what's going on under the hood.

Divergence

The other useful quantity is the divergence. It's the opposite of the gradient and tells you how much a variable changes per time step.

If you're stepping through your neural network, this makes sense: if your value decreases by one and then increases by two, it increases by one per time step. This can be generalized to multiples of two or three: if your value decreases by four, then increase by eight, then it increases four times over its previous value at each step.

Introducing Alpha

A hyperparameter is a neural network parameter that cannot be learned from the data. You can think of it as a constant (or rather, constant-ish) value used to train your model.

The alpha hyperparameter affects how we update our parameters during training and learning. In other words, it tells us how much we should adjust each weight during our gradient descent. It's often set as 0.001 at first but then increased when you get better results until it eventually converges to its optimal value.

The learning rate is one of the most important parameters of a neural network. It determines how quickly you converge to an optimal solution, and it also affects how long it takes your network to learn.

A small alpha means you learn slowly, which is useful for training models that require large amounts of data or time.

A large alpha means you learn quickly but at the cost of overfitting your model on the training set by using too much from it in your gradient descent (i.e., where we're taking steps toward an optimal solution).

Using Alpha in Your Work

Alpha measures how well an agent learns to generalize from its environment. Because it measures how much an agent has learned, it can be used as a learning objective in neural networks.

We can think of alpha as the expected error rate when testing an agent on new data drawn from its environment (potentially modified slightly). This is useful because we might want our agents to be able to predict what will happen in the future based on past experiences and knowledge they've gained over time. Still, we don't necessarily want them to remember every single detail about each experience they've ever had! That would take up too much space in memory and slow down our agents while trying to perform other tasks. So instead, we want our agents able to focus on just enough information so that they can generalize from one situation (or context) into another situation that looks similar enough to us humans.

Code Example

The code example below demonstrates how to create a complete neural network with Alpha In Neural Learning. It uses the MNIST dataset of handwritten digits as an example, a standard benchmark in machine learning research and widely used by researchers worldwide.

You'll need to have Python 3 installed on your computer before doing this project.

- import NumPy as np

- import pandas as pd

- import matplotlib.pyplot as plt

- import tensorflow as tf

- import tensorflow.keras as k

- import tensorflow.contrib.learn as learn

The MNIST dataset consists of a set of 60k images that have been labeled with the correct digit (e.g., 0, 1, 2, ...9). We'll use these labels to train our neural network and then test it on a set of 10k images.

The following code will download the MNIST dataset into a folder called "data" in your home directory:

tensorflow.examples.tutorials.mnist import input_data mnist = input_data.read_data_sets("/home/user/data")

The MNIST dataset consists of a set of 60k images that have been labeled with the correct digit (e.g., 0, 1, 2, ...9). We'll use these labels to train our neural network and then test it on a set of 10k images.

Now that we have our data, let's look at some examples. We can use matplotlib to plot images.

```
show_digit(mnist.train.images[0])
```

For our neural network to work properly, we'll need to convert each image from an array of pixel values in the range [0-1] into a binary matrix (e.g., 0 for black pixels and 1 for white). We'll use this binary matrix as our input data for training and testing.

This code will plot some of these images:

```
fig = plt.figure() for i in range(9):
subplot
```

You Can Use Alpha to Your Advantage

Alpha is a new way of training neural networks. The idea behind alpha is that, instead of using the backpropagation algorithm to adjust weights in each layer of a neural network, we use a more general approach that works with any function. This works especially well for deep learning problems because it's unnecessary to have an explicit representation of your data in memory at each layer; you can just write down your original objective and let alpha figure out how best to solve it.

Alpha has several advantages over backpropagation:

- It can be applied more generally than backpropagation alone, allowing greater flexibility when solving optimization problems with neural networks.

- You don't need to include any special features in the architecture of your models or require any particular initialization scheme (such as random initialization).

Chapter 5

Let's Talk Gradient Descent

This section aims to learn how gradient descent works in a neural network. It generalizes linearly separable problems (like logistic regression or binary classification) to arbitrary functions, which are learned by minimizing the sum of squared errors (SSE).

Gradient Descent

Gradient descent is a general learning algorithm that attempts to minimize the cost function by moving in the opposite direction of the gradient. The objective of this algorithm is to find weights that are associated with a specific point and how they affect other points. To do so, we need to compute the partial derivatives of our cost function at each point (W). Once we have these values, we can use them to update our weight matrices (W) when running gradient descent.

Multiple Inputs

One of the essential concepts in machine learning is the idea that we can learn multiple parameters at once. This is a fundamental concept because it allows us to reduce the times we need to evaluate our model, making training much faster and easier.

This section will review some basic terminology and discuss how you can implement it using OpenAI Gym's "Reinforce" environment. Finally, I'll give an example using Keras so that you can get your hands dirty and see how these algorithms work in action!

Let's start by defining stochastic gradient descent. We'll be using this term throughout the rest of this section, so it's essential to understand what it means!

What is stochastic gradient descent? Stochastic gradient descent (SGD) is an iterative optimization method that seeks to find the minimum of a function by taking small steps in the direction of the steepest descent. It's used in machine learning to optimize parameters such as weights and biases. SGD can be used for supervised learning problems, including classification tasks like image recognition or regression tasks like predicting housing prices. In this section, I will focus on how SGD can be used for training neural networks. For example, if you have a dataset of images of dogs and cats and want to train a model that can identify which type of animal is in an image, SGD will help you find the best values for the weights and biases in your model. The main difference between stochastic gradient descent and gradient descent is how they update their parameters. In stochastic gradient descent, updates are made concerning each training sample (hence why it's called Stochastic). Conversely, in gradient descent, updates are made concerning all samples simultaneously (batch). The difference between stochastic gradient descent and stochastic gradient descent with momentum is how the weights are updated. In SGD with momentum, we update our weights using an exponential moving average of their gradients. This helps us dampen oscillations and escape local minima by applying a force on the moving average when moving in a specific direction. With many features, SGD with momentum can also help you find a better solution faster than traditional SGD. All of this sounds complicated, but it's very straightforward. Like all other machine learning algorithms, SGD comprises simple mathematical operations that perform the computations needed to learn from data.

In this case, the update rule that performs best is the one that moves towards the direction of a tremendous change in the objective function. In other words, if you want to learn faster, use more examples! However, there are some drawbacks to using many samples simultaneously: Larger sample sizes increase memory usage and make processing slower. - It takes a long time to compute gradients for large samples (more than one).

Multiple Outputs

Let's now consider learning a function that maps inputs to outputs.

The function is a neural network whose parameters are also called weights.

The neural network is trained using backpropagation, in which the gradients are calculated for all hidden layers and then used to update the weights of each layer. This process is repeated until sufficient convergence occurs or some stopping criterion is met (e.g., number of iterations).

Finally, gradient descent can be used with multiple output nodes instead of just one. As was done previously when we were only considering binary classification problems like spam detection or handwritten digit recognition tasks where there were two possible outputs (1s and 0s).

In this case, we'll have many more outputs and weights because there are now four categories instead of two. We simply start with some initial values and then use backpropagation to calculate gradients using those parameters to learn these weights.

This means that if we have a set of weights where each weight connects one input node to all output nodes, we can just compute the gradient of the error concerning each weight and update them based on these gradients. This way, our network will be able to learn how much influence any given input has over different outputs.

This is a simple, intuitive way of learning multiple weights at once, which can be useful for understanding how neural networks work and how gradient descent works (since it's essentially the same thing). With this method, you'll see that even though we're only seeing one weight update at a time (in the form of a single gradient vector), we can still use everything we've learned about gradients and their definitions to generalize our approach.

To show this, we'll start again with a simple example. We'll train a network to learn the weights w_1 and w_2 that best fit some training data consisting of only two features (x_1, y_1) and (x_2, y_2). The goal is to extend our loss function by adding these new weights to it so that they don't interfere with the optimization process.

Multiplying two vectors together gives us a scalar. This can be done in many ways, but the most common way is to take the dot product of those vectors (also called a "scalar product"). The dot product is defined as follows:

Where $a * b$ is the dot product of vectors a and b, and a_i and b_i are the ith elements in those two vectors. The trick to making this work is that we must be able to multiply our input vector by the weight vector without any problems arising from dimensionality (thus, we can't simply add another weight). To do this, we need to write our loss function so that multiplying it by the input vector will yield an output.

This is a basic example, but it's super useful because now we can train our network to learn multiple weights simultaneously.

We Will Build a Model Where the Features Are X1 and X2, and the Target Feature Y Is Calculated as Y = F(X1,X2) = 2*X1 + 3*X2

You will use a linear regression model with the features x1 and x2 and target feature y as outputs. The features are multiplied by 2 and 3, respectively, and then added to the y value.

To do this in Python:

```
import NumPy as np

from sklearn import linear_model

X = np.array([[0, 1], [1, 2]]) #
```

The dataset we'll be using has two columns (x1 and x2) which we will multiply by 2 and 3 respectively to calculate our y value (the target feature). You can think of each column as one input variable (e.g., x1 is your first input variable). But in this case, it's more convenient just to think of them as being two separate columns so that we don't have to create an additional column just for storing the output values when they're calculated later on. If that were necessary, though, we could add another column called "y" here

70

instead, containing those same values after multiplying by their respective weights beforehand!

Now that we've got our data set up, let's create three variables to store our feature weights (x1, x2) and the target value (y). These are all initialized at zero because they will be updated using gradient descent when training occurs later.

Now that we've defined our model, let's use the gradient descent function to adjust our weights. The grad_descent function takes three parameters: alpha (the learning rate) and theta (a vector containing initial values for each weight). If you want to update just one of them at a time, then use the index operator (e.g., .[0] or .[1]) followed by assigning it another value such as 0.001 because this won't change anything else.

We call our gradient descent function with two parameters: the learning rate (0.01) and our feature weights (w1 = 0, w2 = 0). We'll store these in a tuple called theta. The gradient descent algorithm should start at iteration number 1, which means we also need to pass that as an argument to our function. Finally, we can use this new value of theta (which contains updated values for each weight) whenever calculating sum_of_squared_-errors again, rather than using the old values. Then we'll update the weights in a loop as often as necessary until they reach some threshold value where they don't change much anymore or if we just want them to stop at one point.

We can see how this works by plotting our actual values against predicted ones with a scatter plot and then drawing lines to represent where each one should be. Then we'll add some text labels for them and finally print out what the RMSE is. This will give us an idea of how accurate our model really is.

Transforming a Single Delta into Three

Now that we've looked at how to get the gradient for a single weight, let's take a step back and see how we can apply these principles to multiple weights in one layer.

Let's say we have an input

```
x_1 = [1 0 1],
```

which results from multiplying two matrices, m_11 and m_22 (the second row of both matrices). The output

```
y=f(x) is [1 2 3].
```

We want to train our network to learn these values more accurately. To do this, we will use Gradient Descent with three separate learning rates—one for each weight and bias in our model:

```
η_w[i] = alpha_w[i] * w[i];

η_{bias} = alpha_{bias}; η_{node} =
max(alpha_wα_{bias})
```

Our task is to find the f(x) gradient for each weight. We can do this by taking the partial derivative of f(x) with respect to each weight, then multiplying by its learning rate:

Since

```
w_2 and w_3 \frac{∂ \text{f}
(\boldsymbol{\text{x}})}{∂ \text{w}_{2}} =
α_{w[2]} * w[2] \frac{∂ \text{f}
(\boldsymbol{\text{x}})}{∂ \text{w}_{3}} =
α_{w[3]} * w[3]
```

Now that we have the gradients for each weight and bias, we can use them to calculate the delta for each weight. The delta for each weight is the product of its learning rate and its gradient:

```
Δw_{i} = α_{w[i]} * w[i]
```

The delta for each bias is just the learning rate multiplied by 1.0 (since it's constant):

```
Δbias = α_{bias}
```

The final step is to multiply this value by the partials

```
\frac{∂ \text{f} (\boldsymbol{\text{x}})}{∂
\text{w}_{1}} = α_{w[1]} * w[1]
```

By doing this, we get the final gradient for each weight.

What Does Freezing a Weight Do?

If you freeze a weight, it will not change. So if you have a network that learns to predict the output of one input and then freezes the first layer (say), what happens? Let's look at an example:

Suppose you have a four-layer network (i.e., a two-hidden-layer network) that predicts whether an image belongs to a certain class.

If you freeze the weights in the first layer, you create a situation in which each neuron in the first layer will receive only one input—the pixel value from its corresponding position on the input image.

You can see how changing the weights in the second layer would affect each neuron in the third layer. But changing weight in the first layer will not affect any other neurons. Thus, when you freeze these weights, you are effectively creating an input image that has been normalized (i.e., transformed) to contain only one value per pixel: either zero or one.

Now, what happens when you freeze another weight? Well, suppose that you freeze a second layer. Then the first two layers are frozen, and each neuron in the third layer has two inputs: the pixel value from its corresponding position on the input image and some other value. We can repeat this process infinitely, always freezing one more layer of weights so that each neuron in the next layer has a new input.

The second input is always the same, so we end up with an infinite number of neurons in the next layer that each has one input—the pixel value from their corresponding position on the input image. What does this mean for our neural network? The answer lies in how neurons process information. As explained earlier, when a neuron receives two inputs from the previous layer, it performs mathematical operations on those inputs to produce an output value for itself. It then passes that output to its next layer of neurons.

You can also freeze a weight when you know that the weight will not change. For example, suppose we freeze some weights but realize that they will all change in one direction or another. If we don't want these values

to change, we'll have to freeze them. This is called "freezing a weight". We can repeat this process infinitely, always freezing one more layer of weights so that each neuron in the next layer has a new input. The second input is always the same, so we end up with an infinite number of neurons in the next layer that each has one input—the pixel value from their corresponding position on the input image.

This Code Freezes the Weights of One Layer

```python
```python

import numpy as np

import matplotlib.pyplot as plt

from sklearn import datasets, models,
metrics, feature_selection, cross_validation

from sklearn.feature_extraction.text import
CountVectorizer

from sklearn.model_selection import
train_test_split

from keras.models import Sequential from
keras.layers import Dense, Dropout
```

Load the weights into a variable called 'weights'. We are going to load them from a file and temporarily freeze them so we can see
```

what they look like before training our model with them - this is just for demonstration purposes!

```
weights = np.loadtxt('weights-filepath',
delimiter=',') weights =
npLayers(weights).freeze() #
```

Create an instance of the model using the frozen weights "layer1".

Use the default values for everything else.

```
layer1 = Sequential() layer1.add(Dense(100))
layer1.add(Dense(10))
```

One Input – Multiple Predictions

You may have noticed that neural networks can make multiple predictions using only a single input. These are called multi-layer neural networks or MLNs. In an MLN with multiple outputs and a single input, the final layer will output multiple values (different classifications).

In contrast, in an MLN with multiple inputs and a single output, there might be many hidden layers between the input data and the final layer. In this case, each hidden layer has one neuron for its previous layers and one for itself. For example, if your image has three channels of color information and two dimensions of spatial position information, then $3 \times 2 = 6$ neurons would be needed per hidden layer). The hidden layers transform your raw data into something more useful for classification purposes by passing it through increasingly complex transformations until you have something that resembles actual classifications from which you can learn from examples and generalize across other instances.

Generalizing Gradient Descent

In this section, we'll look at how to generalize gradient descent so that it can be used to learn any function of many variables.

The key idea is that you can use your knowledge of all the training data points to approximate the derivative of the loss function concerning any particular weight. If you know all this information about every weight in your network, you can compute a gradient for every parameter!

This generalization has some interesting consequences:

It makes learning multiple weights at once easy; instead of needing each weight's own separate error term and set of data points, we only need one combined error term and one set of data points per layer (the output layer). This makes it easy to add additional layers without making our computations more complex. We also get a bonus: having access to an entire vectorized representation for each weight. We're free from constraints on our neural network's number of dimensions (or "node counts"). For example, if our input layer had 100 neurons, but no node dimensionality limit was imposed, then we could use 1000-dimensional activation vectors as input into those same 100 neurons. However, if we had only been able to generate gradients over scalar values instead, this would not have been possible without arbitrarily high memory usage requirements.

What These Weights Learn:

The weights are learning how to make the predictions more accurate.

In other words, they're learning how to reduce error.

Each weight tries to reduce the error when you train a neural network. But what do they learn in aggregate?

How do these individual weights work together to produce a good learning rule?

One way is with weighted sums and dot products. Weighted sums essentially take the average of two inputs and multiply that by some coefficient. Dot products are a similar concept; they multiply two vectors together, but they only work if their lengths match up (e.g., one vector has the same number of elements as another). Both techniques are used here because we can combine them with other techniques like dropout or batch normalization, which change how much weight each input has on our network's output. This affects how much attention each neuron pays towards its neighbors' activities during training time and how much error reduction occurs when improving itself based on those same neighbor signals after being fed through its hidden layers first!

The Code Below Demonstrates How to Perform Gradient Descent on the Sine Function

```
import numpy as np
```

```
import matplotlib.pyplot as plt

def sine(x):

return np.sin(x) - np.cos(x)

def main():

plt.plot(np.linspace(-10, 10, 200))

for i in range (10):

plt.plot(np.linspace(-10, 10, 200),
(i/10)*sine(i/10)) plt.show() if __name__ ==
`__main__': main()
```

Let's take a look at the result: You can see that the sine function has been approximated by a straight line. The gradient descent algorithm will continue to draw more and more straight lines until it converges on a solution.

Visualizing the Weight Values

Visualizing weight values is useful for understanding what the network does.

A weight value of 0 means that this neuron doesn't affect the input – no matter how high you set it, it won't ever be higher than 0. On the other hand, a weight value of 1 means that this neuron has full control over its output through its input – if you set its input to 3, then it will always output 3, regardless of other factors. The middle ground between these two extremes may seem like an insignificant difference from a mathematical standpoint, but there are many interesting applications for learning multiple weights simultaneously (MLAT).

Visualizing weight values is useful for understanding how the network is learning. To visualize how a neural network learns, you need to know what each weight value represents in terms of its connection with other neurons. For example, if the weight from input A goes into the hidden layer on top of B and C, then you can see that this means that A must have at least some effects on B. However, if a neuron's only input comes from another neuron with no connections (or connections to other neurons),

you won't be able to see its effect on any other neuron. For example, if there are no connections between input A and output Z, Z won't be influenced by changes in A. This means that visualizing weight values is useful for understanding how the network is learning.

Visualizing the Weighted Sums, or Dot Products

Now that we have a basic understanding of the gradient descent algorithm, let's talk about how we can visualize what is happening under the hood. Specifically, I want to show you how to visualize dot products as computers compute them.

The dot product is a fundamental operation in mathematics: it's used everywhere, from physics and engineering to machine learning and data science. The dot product takes two vectors (or points) and returns a scalar value (a single number). It measures their similarity by weighting each coordinate with its corresponding weight and summing up those weighted sums. We can easily see this pattern when plotting dots in 3D space:

```python
`` {python}

import matplotlib

import NumPy as np

# create two random vectors with different
weights (0-1) on each dimension

x = np.random.randn(2, 3) +
0j*np.random.randn(3, 1) + 0j*np.random(2)

y = np.random(2).astype(np.float32)*0j +
np.random(-1).astype(np.float32)*0j +
npmatplotlib_setp()matplotlib_show()ax =
plt[5]plt[5].imshow([x],
cmap="gray")plt[5].set_title("X")plt[6].imsh
ow([y], cmap="gray")plt[6].set_title("Y")
```

The gradient descent algorithm is a general learning algorithm that can be used for many different problems. It's a simple and natural generalization of the delta rule. The important thing to remember about gradient descent is that it's not just about prediction; every machine learning model fits into this framework, even if it doesn't involve prediction!

Many people get confused because they think learning means predicting some outcome based on an input. But this isn't true at all! Most models don't even have an output layer! For example:

Linear regression models don't have any outputs - they're just trying to find weights (parameters) so that they can make predictions by making inferences from their inputs using those parameters as coefficients in their expressions (equations).

Neural networks don't have outputs either - they're trying to find weights and biases so that their neurons will respond correctly when presented with some input pattern.

The important thing to remember about gradient descent is that it's not just about prediction; every machine learning model fits into this framework, even if it doesn't involve prediction! This means you don't need to worry too much about whether your problem involves or requires some "output" layer. Instead, find a way to represent the relationship between inputs x1, ..., xn, and whatever you're trying to predict y as some function $f(x1, .., xn) = y$, where f has some parameters (weights and biases) that we want to learn. This can be done for any problem with any type of data or objective (e.g., classification problems, regression problems, etc.) - all you need to do is find a suitable representation!

Stochastic Gradient Descent

Stochastic Gradient Descent (SGD) is a generalization of gradient descent. In SGD, we use an iterative procedure to minimize the cost function with stochastic updates:

Randomly choose a learning rate and an initial weight vector for each iteration.

Compute the gradients of f(x) using the current parameters and weights, and update them according to some rule, e.g.,

```
|w_{i} - w_{i-1}| ^ 2 * learningRate * g(x).
```

This can be simplified as

```
w_{i+1} = w_i - learnRate * g(x).
```

Repeat steps 1-2 until convergence.

Chapter 6

Let's Talk Backpropagation

Deep learning is a rapidly-growing field of artificial intelligence that has the potential to solve some of the world's most pressing problems. But what exactly is it?

A neural network is a system composed of many interconnected processing units (nodes) that work together to solve a specific problem, such as classifying images or recognizing spoken language.

In addition to providing an overview of deep learning and its applications, this piece will explore backpropagation—the primary algorithm used in training feedforward neural networks—and provide some examples of how it works in practice.

Building a Neural Network Using NumPy

Suppose you have the following data set:

```
1 2 3 4 5 6 7 8 9 10 11 12 13 14 15 16 17

0.8 0.3 0.6 -1.4 1.0 0.7 -2.2 1.4 2.9 -0.8 -
1.2 3.5 1..7

0 1 2 4 8 16 32 64 128 256 512 1024 2048 (y)
```

You can import this data using NumPy, which provides many useful numeric operations:

```
import numpy as np

import pandas as PD

In [2]: x = np . array ([[- 0 , 8 , 3 ],[ 0
, 3 , 6 ],[- 1 , 4 , 1 ]]) Out [2]:
array([[[-0., 8., 3.]], [0., 3., 6.]], ]]

In [3]: y = np . array ([[- 0 . , 8 . , 3 ],
...]. cumsum ()) . astype ( int ) Out [3]:
array([[[-10],
```

Activation Functions

The activation function is the non-linear function applied to a layer's output. It returns our desired linear output (or something close to it) from our activation functions.

85

The most commonly used activation function is called sigmoid, which looks like this:

$$y = \sigma(x)$$

This equation converts your input x into an output y with values ranging between 0 and 1, where values closer to 1 indicate a higher likelihood that the neuron will fire (that is, activate or produce an output). This means that when you have no inputs, for example, if you were just applying this formula alone with no previous layers, you would get back 0 everywhere! That makes sense because without any inputs, there's no reason for anything to activate/fire/produce an output; everything must be 0!

Computing the Loss

The loss function is the difference between our target and predicted value for each example. We compute this for every example and then sum up all those losses to get our overall error.

To calculate the loss for a single example, we take the square of our prediction error (the difference between our output and target) and divide it by two. This is because, in deep learning, we want to minimize squared error, not an absolute error; squaring both sides ensures that you can add up your errors to get one big number instead of two smaller ones.

Forward and Backward Propagation in a Single Cycle

Forward and backward propagation is two different methods of simulating the behavior of a neural network. Forward propagation calculates the value of each output node from its input values, while backward propagation calculates how much each input value affects each output value. When you first begin training your neural network, you will use forward and backward propagation together to learn how your model performs in real-time.

Here's an example: Let's say we've trained our network to predict whether or not someone is at risk for heart disease based on their age and height measurements. We feed 100 people of different ages and heights into our model, producing a prediction for each case (true/false).

Now let's say that our model predicted that a certain person was at risk for heart disease when they were not at risk (false positive). When we run backpropagation through this case to see what caused the error, we might find out that one particular feature (age) had an unusually large influence over whether or not someone gets heart disease.

Backpropagation Intuition

Now that we've seen the nuts and bolts of how backpropagation works, let's try to understand it at a high level.

Backpropagation is an iterative process of updating weights in a neural network by propagating the error signal back through the network. This process involves taking partial derivatives (gradients) concerning each weight and passing them through different layers until they reach the output layer. It is essentially a gradient descent optimization technique for finding optimal values for weights in neural networks.

Reshaping Arrays

Reshaping is the process of changing the shape of an array.

This is necessary when you want to feed your neural network input data that is a different size than what it expects. In other words, if you have an input array [30 x 5] and want to feed it into a neural network with two hidden layers requiring input data with dimensions [10 x 100], then reshaping is necessary.

The reshape function in NumPy does this job for us. It takes one or more arrays as arguments, including multi-dimensional arrays (such as 2D matrices) or scalar values (like integers). Using this function will cause each column in your first argument(s) to be extended by padding zeros before and after each value until they reach the desired size:

```Python
import numpy as np

print "Original Shape:" np. shape ( my_input
)

my_input = np . random. And ([ 30, 6 ]) #
Initialize random numbers between 0 - 1 from
NumPy's standard distribution functions

print "After Reshaped Shape:," np. reshape (
my_input , [( 20 , 3 )]) # Reshaping using
list syntax
```

Updating Parameters

Now that you've learned about gradient descent let's look at a more specific algorithm: backpropagation. Backpropagation is an iterative optimization method for finding a parameter vector that minimizes the error in your neural network's output. Remember that we can think of our network as having many different layers—each one takes in some input data, processes it using some function, and produces an output value. Since all these layers are connected (via weights), they can influence each other's outputs by changing their weights slightly. This process is called weight adjustment because it adjusts how much each neuron gives to another neuron's input signal when it computes its output.

The backpropagation algorithm works by repeatedly adjusting these weights based on how much error there is between the actual output and predicted output values (generated from our model's parameters) and how much of this error comes from each layer in our network.

What Are Matrices?

You have probably heard the term matrix before, but you might not be sure what it means. Matrices are similar to arrays in that they store numbers and can be used to perform operations on them. A typical array has rows and columns, but a matrix has rows that contain different types of data (e.g., one column for each feature). You could think of a two-by-two matrix as like four separate arrays: one for each column and another for each row.

So, what are the properties of a good data matrix? First and foremost, it has to have all the right dimensions.

Second, it needs to be large enough for the network to learn from. A network with too few neurons won't be able to learn much; one with too many may suffer from overfitting (i.e., not generalizing).

Third—and perhaps one of the most important parts—it must mimic the outside world well enough that your model can make accurate predictions about things like images, text, or audio clips. If these predictions aren't accurate enough (that is, if they're too far away from reality), then your model won't work well in production settings. However: how do we know whether our models are accurate? How do we know they're doing what we want them to do?

Suppose you have a table with four rows and three columns (4 x 3). You want to represent the following information about your table: "the first row contains the numbers 0 - 3; the second row contains the numbers 4 - 7; column 1 has no entries." This can be done by creating a matrix that looks like this:

```
(0,4)  (1,5)  (2,6)  (3,7)
```

Full, Batch, and Stochastic Gradient Descent

There are three ways to train a neural network using backpropagation: full gradient descent, batch gradient descent, and stochastic gradient descent. Each uses the same method of updating weights but makes different assumptions about how many examples should be used simultaneously.

Full Gradient Descent: This method trains the model on your training data at once. It's called "full" because it uses the entire dataset for every training iteration. As a result, you'll have to store all of your data in memory or disk—or both—and then create new models in parallel until they converge on good results (i.e., when they start getting closer to their targets).

Learning Correlation

Deep Neural Networks learn correlation by stacking layers on top of each other. The first layer is called an input layer because it represents the inputs to the rest of your model. Then you can add more layers representing hidden states and another layer representing outputs. The additional inputs are optional and are called bias units, which don't contribute any additional information but simply help focus your network's attention where it should be so that it can learn faster.

The way this works is by using a technique called Stacking Neural Networks or Encoder-Decoder Layers (EDLs)

Up and Down Pressure

To calculate the up and down pressure, we need a loss function. The loss function measures how far away our current output is from what we want to achieve. For example, if you're trying to predict whether or not someone will purchase your product, then your loss function might be the sum of squared errors (i.e., how much you were off in each prediction).

If you've taken calculus before, this concept should be very familiar—it's exactly how we calculate derivatives! If you haven't taken calculus before and don't quite understand why finding the derivative of an equation helps us find its slope, read on! The basic idea here is that we can use derivatives to determine how quickly things change in various parts of our equations at specific points in time.

Example 1

In this first example, we will be calculating the loss function for two different scenarios. We will be using the same inputs but with different outputs. This shows how the loss function changes depending on whether the output is what we are looking for. In this case, our input variables are:

A: Amount of coins in your pocket before buying a candy bar from a vending machine

B: Amount of coins you have left after buying a candy bar from a vending machine

Our loss function will be defined as The difference between the number of coins you had before buying your candy bar multiplied by 100 and the number of coins you have left after buying your candy bar. In other words, if your pocket contained 100 coins and now only contains 50 coins, then this would be considered a "loss" because it's not what we're looking for. We may also want to subtract this value from 1 to get an idea of how close or far away we are from achieving our goal. In this case, the loss function would be: (1-0.5)*100 = 50. If our pocket originally had 100 coins and now contains 150 coins, then this would be considered a "gain" because it's what we're looking for! Our new loss function would be: $(1+0.5)*100 = 150$.

Example 2

In this example, we will use a loss function that produces both up and down pressure. The general form of this loss function is:

```
L(y,f(x)) = (1 - y)my + ym-1 f(x), for some
m ∈ N
```

The loss function is an increasing function of the prediction when the true label is 0 but a decreasing function of the prediction when the true label is 1. In other words, this loss function penalizes incorrect predictions more heavily than correct predictions.

The penalty for incorrect predictions is more severe when the true label is 0 and less severe when the true label is 1. If we use a perfect predictor (f(x)=1), this loss function penalizes incorrectly predicting 1s.

We can use this loss function to show that it produces both up and down pressure. Let's start by considering the directional derivative of the loss at some point x0 where f(x) = 0.

As before, we can use the directional derivative of the loss function in a particular direction to formulate an update rule for the predictor. For example, if we want to maximize the loss along some direction s then we would update our predictor according to

```
f(x) ← f(x) - ε · ∇L(y,f(x)) ·s.
```

It turns out that for this particular loss function,

```
∇L(0,f(x)) · s = 0 for any direction s.
```

This means that we cannot progress in maximizing the loss in a particular direction since its directional derivative vanishes.

Let's now consider what happens if we try to minimize the loss in a particular direction. In this case, we would update our predictor according to:

```
f(x) ← f(x) - ε · ∇L(1,f(x))·s.
```

Let's assume that the label is 1, and we want to minimize the loss in some direction s. To do this, we need to compute:

```
∇L(1,f(x)) · s.
```

We can compute this quantity by differentiating the loss function with respect to f(x) and then multiplying by s:

```
∇L(1,f(x))·s = -∇L(1,f(x))·s = -log (1/(1 +
exp (-f(x)= log (1/(1 + exp (-f(x))) · s =
-log (exp (-f(x))/ (exp (-f(x+ 1)) · s =
-f(x) · s.
```

This means that in any direction s, the loss increases as you decrease f(x). What does this mean? It means there is no way to minimize the loss by moving f(x) in any direction. If you move it up or down, then the loss will increase.

Overfitting

The most important thing to remember is that deep neural networks can overfit your data. Overfitting can be caused by having too many parameters or by not having enough training examples. Unfortunately, it's easy for even the simplest neural networks to overfit, so it pays to be careful in this regard when designing your model.

To prevent overfitting, you should use regularization on your deep learning algorithm. Regularization refers to machine learning methods that help avoid overfitting by penalizing certain kinds of behavior from your model during training. Applying these techniques differs depending on the network architecture you are working with and what kind of data set you are trying to analyze. For example:

Dropout regularization involves removing random units (or "neurons") from the hidden layers during training to reduce computation costs while preserving information about those neurons' inputs and outputs;

L2 regularized logistic regression involves adding a penalty term equal (+/-1) times an L2 norm between two vectors' weights at each iteration;

Conflicting Pressure

You might be wondering what to do if the error is too large. This can happen when the gradient is too high or low or if your data is noisy. The most likely cause of large errors is that you are using too many features (or not enough), so try reducing the number of features used in a prediction and see how that changes things.

If your error seems to fluctuate wildly, it may mean that your model's weights don't match what they're supposed to represent— perhaps they are learning different things than they should be learning! For example, if you train two identical models on two separate datasets but use different random seeds for each. Since these seeds determine how training proceeds at every step up until this point, changing them drastically changes what gets learned (and, by extension, which weights end up with certain values).

How to Create Correlation

Correlation is a measure of the relationship between two things. In this case, we will use correlation to measure how well our neural network can fit an input signal with its output signal.

Correlation is a way of measuring how much two things change together. The higher the correlation, the more closely related the two data points are. If you were trying to predict how much rain will fall tomorrow by looking at today's weather conditions and comparing that against historical rainfall data for your area, then you would want those numbers to have a high correlation. If it rains today, there's a good chance it will also rain tomorrow!

Stacking Neural Networks

Stacking neural networks is a technique for improving the performance of a neural network. It's a form of feature learning, data compression, and dimensionality reduction. This can be done in various ways, but we'll focus on stacking networks with an L2 weight penalty and an L2 regularization term on the activations (or outputs).

Stacking neural networks like this is fairly simple to implement with Keras' stack module. All you need are three layers: input layer(s), hidden layer(s), and output layer(s). The first parameter passed into each layer is the number of stacked nodes, commonly referred to as "depth." The second parameter passed into each layer specifies whether or not you want L2 regularization applied to those nodes (which we'll discuss later).

Here's what it looks like when you instantiate these layers:

```Python
# Add input layers

layer_input =
InputLayer(num_features=num_features)
```

Backpropagation is the only way to compute the error.

It's used to update the parameters, and thus it's also used to update the weights and biases.

Note that this is a very important point: For backpropagation to work correctly, you must ensure that your neural network has an architecture where each layer is fully connected (or at least fully connected by some hidden units). This is because any type of convolutional neural network uses kernels that apply over multiple values at once – if you have a kernel with 3x3 applied on top of 4 inputs, you'll get 12; outputs after applying a single convolution operator!

Why Does Backpropagation Work?

It's not essential to understand backpropagation at all! But it helps to provide context for why we need derivatives in the first place—and what they're good for (spoiler: they help us train our networks faster).

Linear vs. Nonlinear

We'll use the linear model as an example to show how backpropagation works.

Linear regression is a simple form of supervised learning, where the target value is a continuous number (like millions of dollars), and the input data consists of numbers that are also continuous (such as age, income level, and so on).

For example, we want to predict what someone's salary will be by looking at their age, gender, and education level (all numerical values). The simplest way would be just to add up all these variables' values and use them as inputs for our prediction function, spit out your projected salary. In other words:

$$y = \sum_{i=1}^{n} x_{i}$$

The problem with this approach is that it will always return an average value rather than individualized predictions based on each person's unique set of personal characteristics. As a result, more advanced models, such as logistic regression or neural networks with multiple hidden layers (or "hidden units"), were developed.

'So why is your neural network not working?

You might think, "maybe I've been doing something wrong." After all, you have a big enough dataset of images and their corresponding labels, you are using backpropagation through time (BPTT), and everything is set up correctly. But unfortunately, there is still one major problem: the neural network may be learning too little or too much.

Backpropagation in Code

You'll need to import some libraries to build a deep neural network. In this case, we will use NumPy and Pandas for data manipulation, Matplotlib for plotting, and Ticker for handling date-time objects.

To start with the basics of building a neural network in Python, let's get into the steps:

Step 1 - Initialize Parameters

The first step is to initialize your parameters. You will want to do this at the beginning of every training iteration because it's a good idea to use a different random seed every time you run your model. This ensures it won't be affected by any sort of bias from the data set itself. To do so, simply call init() on all Keras' base layers, which should be done before calling fit().

```python
```

```
#import numpy as np

#import keras

#import pandas as pd

#import matplotlib.pyplot as plt
```

Note that this step isn't necessary unless you'd like to use Keras or PyTorch, which will be needed for both the training and testing phases (i.e., when calling fit()). If you're using a custom framework like Tensorflow or Caffe, skip ahead.

Step 2 - Loop

In the loop, you feed your training data into the network, and it will calculate the output. The network then compares that output with what was expected and calculates a cost. Then, it updates its parameters so they can be used in future iterations of this loop. This process is repeated hundreds or thousands of times until you have enough iterations to get an acceptable result (i.e., when your cost function stops improving).

Step 3 - Calculate Cost

Calculate the cost of your model, which is defined as follows:

```
Cost = (Actual Output - Predicted Output) *
100
```

The actual output is the value you want to predict. For example, if you're trying to predict whether a patient has cancer, then your actual output would be either 1 if they have cancer or 0 if they don't. The predicted output refers to what your neural network predicts for this same prediction data-set. To determine how accurate your neural network's predictions are compared against its desired outputs, calculate the difference between these two values:

```
Actual-Predicted = Actual Output - Predicted
Output
```

Now that you know the actual output and predicted output, you can use this formula to calculate the cost of your model:

```
Cost = (Actual Output - Predicted Output) *
100.
```

This will tell us how close our predicted output was to its desired result. If there is a match between these two values, then the cost will be zero (or near zero). This means we have accurately identified whether or not a patient has cancer.

Step 4 - Backward Propagation

You have just calculated the gradients of the loss function, so you can now use these to calculate the error.

For example:

```
` ` `

if a == 1:

if b == 2:

if c == 3:
```

```
# this is an error because there isn't an
element with value 4 in A[0][1][2]

```

``` if a == 1: if b == 2: if c != 3:
```

The error is then calculated by multiplying the gradient and the loss function value:

``` ```err = loss_function * gradients```.

This may seem like a lot to take in at first, but after you have done it a few times, you will find it easy to understand.

Step 5 - Update Parameters

The last step is to update the parameters using gradient descent. Gradient descent is a method for updating parameters by taking steps toward the steepest descent. This means that we're trying to get closer to the optimal value for our parameter values, and thus we'll try different values until we find ones that work best.

In this case, we will be using backpropagation as our training method instead of gradient descent because it's more efficient and accurate when training deep neural networks (DNNs), which are used in many applications such as image recognition or speech recognition.

The process of backpropagation is a complex one, so this section is going to be relatively short. Here's how it works:
```

The goal of training a neural network is to minimize the loss of function. This means that we want to find values for the parameters (weights and biases) such that they correctly predict what we know about our inputs and outputs.

The loss function penalizes mistakes made by the network in its predictions—it usually has two components: a prediction error term and an error term related to how close the system was to predicting the correct output values. These are functions of all the weights and biases in your neural network, so they help you determine which parameters need tweaking during training if things aren't working out as well as expected!

Why Deep Networks Are Important

Deep neural networks are a subset of machine learning, a subfield of artificial intelligence. Machine learning is the field that studies how to make computers do things that currently require human intelligence. Deep learning is a subset of machine learning and artificial intelligence (AI).

AI typically refers to systems that exhibit "artificial general intelligence" (AGI), able to perform any intellectual task that a human can. Humans have this ability because our brains contain millions of neurons connected in intricate ways; however, we can only comprehend what's going on inside our brains by introspection- meaning we're missing out on all sorts of useful information; about our minds! Even if you don't consider yourself an AI researcher or enthusiast, you probably interact with some form daily: your GPS app uses AI; your digital assistant at work uses it; even Siri has been programmed using deep neural networks!

Why Create Intermediate Datasets with Correlation?

The purpose of creating intermediate datasets that correlate is to create a network that is more efficient and can learn more effectively. This creates a network that can learn more effectively than a network with no correlation.

Deep learning frameworks (like Keras, TensorFlow, PyTorch, etc.) have a lot of advantages, including fast computation, highly efficient memory access, and easy-to-use APIs.

It is important to note that this type of neural network model is not the only one out there. There are many other types of deep learning networks, each with its strengths and weaknesses. For instance, convolutional neural networks are designed for image recognition and have different layers than regular feedforward nets.

Deep learning is an exciting field, and the future is bright.

Chapter 7

Introducing Regularization and Batching

W e'll look at how our simple neural network deals with noise in its training set: a sample from real-world data sets will always be "noisy" or imperfect by design.

Overfitting

Overfitting is when a model is too complex and doesn't generalize well. Overfitting happens when your model cannot adapt to changes in the data and learn from new information. It also occurs when you use too many features, which can be problematic if you have limited data or don't know what features are essential for making predictions.

Overfitting can be an issue in healthcare modeling because data are expensive, and analysis is high stakes. The most common reasons machine learning models fail include overfitting (and, even worse: underfitting).

Memorization vs. Generalization

There is a difference between memorization and generalization. It's easy to tell if your model memorizes: it will perform the same on every problem in a given data set. This can occur when you use too much regularization or an overly complicated model. On the other hand, a generalization error may look like randomness—your model will perform well on some problems but poorly on others in the same data set.

Generalizing well depends more heavily on how many examples you're training with than how complex your model is (although complexity matters too). So what's the best way to get better at generalizing? Batch sizes!

Batch sizes are like a safety net for generalization. If your model only repeatedly sees the same 20 problems, it will memorize them quickly. But if you use different batch sizes (say, 5 to 100), generalization improves on test data! For example, if you're trying to predict what a person will order based on their previous orders at restaurants or stores—but they haven't ordered anything yet—then using batches of 1 would give you better results than multiple batches.

Don't Overtrain Your Neural Networks

The previous section discussed how neural networks could get worse if you train them too much. This phenomenon is called overfitting and occurs when a model learns the training data too well. In other words, it fits the noise in your data as well as possible but does not generalize well to new data.

Overfitting can be particularly problematic for deep learning models because they're designed to learn lots of features simultaneously and correlate them with each other (this is why they can do so well at image classification tasks). These correlated features may exist because there are actual correlations between them or because they were randomly assigned during training (i.e., they aren't related). Because deep networks learn these correlated features, an overfit model will have trouble generalizing well to new examples where some random correlations are no longer true (for example, if you change your image size slightly).

What Causes Overfitting?

Neural networks have proven to be an effective tool for modeling complex data but tend to overfit. Overfitting happens when your model learns the noise in your data rather than anything useful.

One way neural networks can overfit is by memorizing the training examples instead of generalizing them. That's why regularization and batching are critical for preventing this problem from happening during training!

We must be careful not to get too excited about our model's performance during training. We have an excellent chance of overfitting the training data if we don't use a regularization technique like batching or dropout. Try using regularization methods in your next project!

There are many ways to reduce overfitting, but we'll focus on two that are critical for neural networks: regularization and batching. These techniques work well together because they penalize the model for making incorrect predictions about new data.

The first thing you need to know about preventing overfitting is that it occurs when your model learns the noise in your data rather than anything useful. In other words, if your training examples don't provide enough information about what a general prediction should look like, it might be hard for them to generalize well.

Second, you should know that it's possible to improve generalization using regularization methods.

Regularization

Regularization is a technique that helps us prevent overfitting. Overfitting occurs when a machine learning model learns to fit the details of the training data rather than generalizing well to new data.

Regularization prevents this by adding penalties to the objective function of our model.

Regularization can be thought of as an additional term added to our loss function, which we can define in terms of minimizing squared errors:

$L=(y-\hat{y})^2+R(w)$

where y is the true data value and $\hat{y}$ is the predicted value. R(w) is the regularization term, where w is our model weights.

The simplest way to introduce regularization is by adding a penalty on the magnitude of the weights. In other words, we add a term that penalizes large weights. This is called L1 or Lasso regularization:

$R(w)=C\sum_i|w_i|$ where C is a constant.

The intuition behind this equation is that we want our model to use many weights close to zero and few very large weights.

The effect of this penalty is that our network will learn those parameters that are important to the process, while the rest of the weights will be ignored. This will automatically remove redundant components and perform a kind of feature selection. However, in practice, we need to tune a parameter called lambda that controls the amount of regularization. Smaller values mean more regularization and vice versa.

Now let's see this in action. First, we'll use the same model as before—a simple neural network with one hidden layer. Well then, we'll train it on the MNIST dataset and compare the performance of a few different approaches using L1 regularization.

This very simple technique can be combined with any loss function. In our case, we'll use it in conjunction with the loss function introduced in the previous section. To add regularization to this problem, we'll use an extension called L2 regularization or Ridge Regularization:

$R(w)=C\sum_i w_i^2$

Where C is a parameter that controls the amount of regularization, notice that we sum up every weight in our network.

The code for our regularized model is very similar to what we did for batching, only now we use L1 instead of L2 as the cost function. Here are the results:

Hyperparameter | SoftMax cross-entropy | L1 regularization | L2 regularization (batching)

We can see that regularization gives us a lift over baseline, but batching performs even better. The reason is that batching reduces the variance of our estimates, which is not exclusive to regularization. They can be used in combination and are often combined with other techniques!

Early Stopping

Early stopping is a technique for regularization. It's simple and effective but only works well in some cases. To understand why we need to look at the way early stopping works.

In early stopping, we train our model until the loss function stops decreasing (or increases). When this happens, we stop training and report our final model, ready for predictions on new data.

The intuition behind early stopping is that when your model has learned enough about your training set, its performance on new data will not improve much more. If it improves, you have probably overfitted your dataset by finding patterns specific to the examples in your training set but do not generalize well beyond them.

This is a useful technique for models with a large number of parameters. In these cases, it takes longer to train the model, and early stopping can help prevent overfitting without sacrificing too much performance on new data.

However, early stopping is not as effective in problems with a small number of parameters. This is because the training time is already so short that there isn't much opportunity for overfitting to happen. In these cases, another regularization technique might be needed.

Early stopping is a simple regularization that stops the training process when your validation loss function starts to increase. It's most useful for models with many parameters because these take longer to train, and there is more opportunity for overfitting. Early stopping can prevent overfitting without sacrificing too much performance on new data in problems with a smaller number of parameters.

Stop Training!

If you've made it this far in the tutorial, you've probably noticed that there are two ways to stop training a neural network: by setting an error tolerance or by using an early stopping condition.

When you use an error tolerance and continue training until your model reaches that level of accuracy, you risk overfitting the training data. This means your model will perform well on the same dataset but not work well on new data!

An early stopping condition is a way to avoid this pitfall. We're ensuring that our model generalizes well beyond its training set by stopping when performance starts decreasing or plateauing.

You can use the early stopping condition to stop training in three ways:

- Stop training when the error rate starts to increase.

- Stop training when the error rate starts to plateau.

- Stop training when the error rate starts to decrease.

Dropout

One of the most popular regularization techniques is a dropout, which randomly removes units from the network. This helps prevent overfitting and ensures that the network doesn't memorize the training data.

Dropout works by dropping a percentage of units at each training step (e.g., 20%). You then have to predict what these hidden neurons would have produced had they not been dropped out during training. This cross-entropy cost function can then be used for learning and optimization, just like in vanilla neural nets.

Now that you've seen another regularization technique, let's discuss a sampling strategy called batching. We have already discussed feeding data into neural networks in small batches. Let's investigate how this works.

Example of Dropout

Let's take a look at how to apply dropout in your model.

Dropout can be applied on any layer of your neural network, but it's most commonly used on dense layers (i.e., fully connected layers). When applied to a dense layer, dropout essentially consists of randomly setting some of the weights to zero during training and testing like so:

```
\begin{equation} y_t = f(x_1^{(1)},
x_{2^{(2)}}, ... , x_{n^{(n)}} \times W_{1},
b_{1}) \\

y_t \leftarrow y_t + z^{(0)} \end{equation}

where $z^{(0)}$ is the observed output and
$y_t$ is the predicted output at time step
$\text{T}$.
```

Batching

If we use a backdrop to compute the gradient, we have to feed one sample of data at a time. This can be very computationally expensive if your dataset is large. An alternative is batching, which divides the data into smaller sets, often called batches. For example, let's say you have 100 samples of data and want to divide them into 10 batches: each batch would contain 10 samples of data. We now calculate the gradients for each batch separately and update the weights. The average of these gradients will then be used to update the weights. This is called stochastic gradient descent and is a popular way of updating weights in neural networks that use backpropagation.

The advantages of batching are that the computation is reduced, but the downside is that you may not get the exact gradient. At this point, you are probably wondering why we would want to use batching instead of just using backpropagation. Batching allows us to edit the gradients and increase or decrease how much they affect the weight updates. Using backpropagation to train a neural network is often very computationally expensive.

A simple example of this is called dropout. Dropout is a technique to reduce overfitting, or the network memorizing the training data by reducing the number of connections between neurons. The idea behind dropout is that we remove a portion of neurons from the network at each iteration and train just on those remaining.

For example, if we have a network with three layers and 100 neurons at each layer, we could remove 50 of those neurons with dropout. The way this would work is that we would randomly choose 50 of the neurons to remove and keep the other 50 around. We would then train on just those remaining neurons.

Dropout (The L1 Regularizer)

The next regularization technique we will look at is a dropout. A dropout is a form of regularization that randomly drops nodes from the network during training. This technique can be used to prevent overfitting, and it does so by introducing a form of regularization that introduces variance into how each neuron is connected to others.

When you implement dropout, the number of neurons dropped from the network can vary. This variation introduces randomness into how those neurons are connected to others, which prevents overfitting.

One of the most important aspects of regularization is that it's a technique that can be used to prevent overfitting. This is because regularization forces model parameters to be small and prevent them from growing too large. This prevents overfitting because larger model parameters lead to more complex models that don't generalize well on new data.

Dropout and Ensembling

There are two main reasons why dropout works: ensemble learning and regularization. Ensemble learning is training multiple neural nets and combining their predictions to get a better one than any individual network could produce. Dropout regularizes your network by encouraging each node to learn something different from its neighbors, preventing them from memorizing the training data instead of generalizing it. That way, as long as at least one node hasn't been dropped out in a particular layer, that layer can still contribute useful information to the final prediction – even if other layers in between have been completely removed!

This way, we can avoid overfitting our training data while still getting good predictions on new data. Furthermore, we don't need thousands or millions of examples before our model becomes useful (like many deep learning models require).

Using Dropout in the Real World.

Dropout is a regularization technique, which means it's used to reduce overfitting. Overfitting is when your model is too specific to the training data and can't generalize well to new data.

Dropout works by randomly dropping out neurons during training and then taking averages of all these copies of the network to get an idea of how the network behaves without those neurons being present. The resulting averaged graph can be considered a lower-dimensional representation of your high-dimensional space. However, it still captures meaningful information about your original space because it retains some similar underlying structure without redundancy from having multiple identical copies of individual neurons (which tends to happen when you use dropout).

Dropout is a type of regularization and a type of ensembling. It's popular because it's easy to implement and uses many different neural networks.

Even though dropout is a simple technique, it's still important to understand how it works so that you can use it correctly on your machine learning projects. For example, dropout is often used in neural networks with fully connected layers (meaning there's no convolution involved) and in the output layer of classification tasks.

Batch Normalization

Batch Normalization is a simple technique that can dramatically improve the accuracy of your models, especially if you're dealing with neural networks. It is based on the observation that training a neural network can cause internal parameters to become more correlated as learning progresses. This can cause problems for certain neural networks, such as RNNs and LSTMs.

The Batch Normalization layer in Keras is designed to address these problems. It normalizes the output of each layer in a network by scaling it up or down to have a mean value of zero and a standard deviation of one. The layer also performs regularization, which helps prevent overfitting, and creates an output that is easier to learn from

Batching

- Batch normalization is a technique used in deep learning to improve the training of neural networks.

- It helps reduce overfitting and improve generalization.

- It is usually implemented by applying a normalization layer after every convolutional or fully connected layer, but it can also be applied before or between layers.

In Most Real-World Machine Learning Problems, Data Is Noisy and Complex. This Is Especially True in Healthcare Modeling, Where Data Are Expensive to Collect, and Analysis Is High-Stakes. So How Can We Learn the Signal in Our Data?

In healthcare modeling, the cost of collecting data is high. For example: if you want to train a machine learning model that predicts how long someone will be hospitalized for acute kidney failure (AKF), you'd need to measure how sick each individual is. And one way to do this might be with patient surveys or other self-reported measures (like whether or not they're experiencing nausea). But these kinds of data can be unreliable because people may not know how bad off they are—or maybe they don't want others to know because it's embarrassing! Moreover, when your job depends on getting this kind of information right, missing out on even one piece could have dire consequences. For example, if you misclassify someone as having only mild symptoms when they have severe ones, their chances of recovery could plummet—and that's no good for anyone involved!

The answer is simple: Regularization and Batching. These two tools will help you improve your ML models and make them more accurate.

Chapter 8

Probabilities and Nonlinearities with Activation Functions

Activation functions are used for modeling nonlinearities in a neural network. They can be applied at the neural network's hidden or output layer.

What Is an Activation Function?

The purpose of an activation function is to transform the input values into a different representation.

For example, by using a Sigmoid function, you can create a neural network that learns to recognize handwritten digits (see below).

The activation function is a nonlinear function that transforms the input values into a different representation.

Why Do We Need Activation Functions?

In a neural network, the output of one layer is fed into another layer. In this way, the inputs are passed through several layers where they are processed and transformed into outputs. This transformation process can be modeled as a function:

```
In mathematics, f (x) = x + 1
```

But the output from a layer may have a different range of values, and it may not be appropriate to feed them directly into another layer. For example, in some cases, the input values are greater than 1 or less than 0. For example, suppose you want to use f (x) as an activation function for your neural network. In this case, it would not be wise to pass all of x's outputs through another layer because they would end up having values outside what is expected by the

layer that receives the output. To fix this, we introduce an activation function that will scale the values of x to be between 0 and 1. This is what activation functions do: They take an input and transform it into a value between 0 and 1. Of course, some of them may still

121

have the same sign, which means they could still be negative or positive, but we won't have values outside what another layer expects. This makes it possible to use f (x) as an activation function for your neural network.

Introduction to Activation Functions

The activation function is an important part of a neural network and its complexity. The activation function determines how the input is modified and passed to subsequent layers. Activation functions are used in every layer except for the first one, which only takes in raw input values (and thus does not need an activation function). Activation functions can be divided into two main categories: linear and nonlinear.

Constraint 1: Functions Should Be Continuous and Infinite

A continuous function is a function that can be drawn without breaking the graph. On the other hand, a discrete function must be made up of many small steps to approximate it; this is useful when we want to know what happens at every small change in input (think of how you might approximate a sine curve).

An infinite function is also called an "infinite series" or just "series." It is defined as 'the sum of all numbers from 1 up until infinity.' So if you have an infinite series with terms like $2 + 2 + 2 + 2 + ...$ then each term will have an exponent greater than 1 ($2n+1$). Or if you have a series like $x^2 * 1/x * x^3 *...$ then each term will have an exponent less than 1 ($-1 < x < 0$).

Constraint 2: They Must Be Monotonic – They Only Go in One Direction

A function is monotonic if it never changes direction. It's the same as saying that its slope is always positive (or negative) and that it never changes sign.

This is the second constraint on good activation functions. Again it's easy to see why this might be useful. If the slope of an activation function never changes, then it's like saying that we can always trust one direction, two, or three, all at once. This means that when a neuron fires along one of those directions (for example), we know that no other neuron in our network will ever fire along that same direction.

Constraint 3: They Must Be Nonlinear

We need to use nonlinear functions to make a neural network more complex and powerful. A linear function produces a straight line on the graph. A nonlinear function squiggles or turns in some way, allowing it to have more complexity than a simple straight line.

This is because nonlinearity allows for much more flexibility in modeling data and making decisions about what should happen next. Nonlinear functions can be sensitive to inputs in ways that linear ones cannot. It also means that nonlinearly trained neural networks are better at generalizing their training data because they're inherently more flexible than linearly trained networks.

Nonlinear activation functions are more difficult to learn than linear ones because there are many possible shapes of curves rather than just one like with linear activation functions (this is called "overfitting"). But once we get past this initial difficulty using powerful but complex models becomes easier because our ability to generalize increases greatly (see Constraint 4).

Constraint 4: They Must Be Efficiently Computable.

Nonlinearities are everywhere in the world; therefore, it makes sense to model nonlinearities with nonlinear functions. It turns out that some of these functions are much easier to work with than others. For example, suppose you want to do something like computing the derivative of a function $f(x)$ at point x.

In that case, you're going to want your activation function to satisfy certain properties:

If it's differentiable (and we'll call this property monotonicity):

```
\(f' (a)\) is always greater than or equal
to zero for all acceptable values of \(a\)
```

If it's continuous: $f(x+h) - f(x)$ has no jumps when h is small enough.

Both of these things are necessary for computing the derivative of a function.

Standard Hidden-Layer Activation Functions

You can think of a neuron's standard activation function as a function that maps the weighted sum of its inputs to a value between 0 and 1. The most common activation functions are sigmoid, tanh, and ReLU. For example:

The sigmoid activation function is defined by

$$ f(x) = \frac{1}{1+e^{-x}}$$

The sigmoid is often used to model probability distributions because it has an output range between 0 and 1 (the same as saying that it takes values in [0, 1]). It's also used for multilayer perceptrons because when used as an input layer's activation function, it increases signal strength through each layer without saturating or exploding too much at any particular point. In other words: it performs well despite being nonlinear!

Examples of popular activation functions

You can use your custom activation functions, but most of the time, you will want to use one of the following:

- Sigmoid/Logistic (tanh)

- ReLu (Rectified Linear Unit)

- SoftMax Function (standard output layer activation functions)

Sigmoid/Logistic

The sigmoid function is a nonlinear transformation of the input data. It maps the input to a value between 0 and 1, but with a curve that looks like this:

It's called logistic because it's the logistic function, which you may remember from statistics class as being used to model probability distributions. So why not just call it "logistic," then? However, because logistic is also used as an adjective (as in "logistic regression"), calling our activation function by that name would result in confusion.

The sigmoid function got its name because of how its graph resembles an S when viewed from above:

Its mathematical form is, where x is the input data. We can implement it in Python as follows:

```
def sigmoid(x): return 1.0 / (1 + np.exp(-
x))
```

Let's look at what happens when we pass it to some input data: The sigmoid function is monotonic, which always increases or decreases but never oscillates. The sigmoid function is continuous and differentiable, with an S-shaped curve allowing efficient optimization. It's used in the output layer of many classification algorithms such as logistic regression (obviously) and artificial neural networks.

The sigmoid function is also a special case of the more general logistic function. The logistic function is defined as where L, k, and x0 are constants we can set to meet our specific needs. Different choices for these parameters produce different shapes for the curve, but all are S-shaped and closely resemble each other. Because the sigmoid function is monotonic, it can be inverted using a simple lookup table. We simply need to store several points on the curve and then use those to approximate the inverse function. In practice, this is often done with a lookup table that's relatively small because there are only so many discrete values we can store on a computer. This technique is fast and efficient, but if you need more precision, it's easy to compute an actual inverse function using calculus.

Tanh (Hyperbolic Tangent)

Tanh is a non-saturating function. It's defined as the hyperbolic tangent of x, and it's a smoothing function, which means that its output ranges from -0 to +1. This can be useful for modeling probabilities in neural networks since probability distributions are often modeled with Gaussian functions. Since tanh is an element-wise nonlinearity and not an activation function like sigmoid or ReLU, I'll just show you how you would use this at each layer of your neural network:

```
Input Layer: tanh(x) = f(x) = \(
\tanh(\frac{x}{2})\)

Hidden Layer 1: tanh(tanh(y)) = h1

Hidden Layer 2: tanh(tanh(tanh(y))) = h2
```

It's important to note that tanh is often used with other activation functions, like ReLU. For example, if you're building deep neural networks, we recommend using tanh as your final hidden layer activation function, which will convert output values into a range between -1 and +1. Then use ReLU as the first hidden layer

127

activation function, which will convert input values into a range between 0 and 1.

ReLu (Rectified Linear Unit)

ReLu (Rectified Linear Unit): The rectified linear unit is a nonlinear activation function that is modified by the sigmoid function. It has a range of 0 to 1, and it's used in neural networks to solve the vanishing gradient problem.

Image: The ReLu function is commonly used as an activation function for calculating probabilities in classification problems.

It's also known as an activation function and can be used for any type of neural network. For example, it's useful for classification problems such as detecting fraud or spam email because it helps determine whether something is likely a positive or negative outcome. However, ReLu has one disadvantage compared to other activation functions: Its limited output range.

SoftMax Function

The SoftMax function is a common activation function used for classification problems. It maps an output probability distribution into a normal distribution with unit variance, which can then be normalized to 1 (i.e., each element in this new vector should add up to 1). This allows us to use gradient descent on our neural network's weights and inputs to train it using backpropagation algorithms like stochastic gradient descent (SGD).

Standard Output Layer Activation Functions

The SoftMax function predicts the probability of belonging to a particular class.

Imagine that you are training an MLP to classify images of cats and dogs. The input layer has two nodes for each image in the training set, one for cats and one for dogs. The output layer also has two nodes, one for each class: cat or dog (or simply 0 and 1). Now, suppose that you have trained your network to successfully predict whether an image contains a cat or a dog with 90% accuracy. This means its outputs should be close to 0 in cases where there are no cats/dogs in an image (because they will not be classified correctly) and close to 1 when there are cats/dogs present (because they will). The SoftMax function takes these values as input and returns their logits which correspond directly with actual probabilities:

Choosing the best activation function for your model depends on what you're trying to predict.

Activation functions are useful for modeling nonlinearities, probabilities, and classifications.

Configuration 1: No Activation Function – Prediction of Raw Values

No activation function: The most common model is a regression model, which predicts one target value for each input. Regression models can be trained using the same learning algorithms for classification models (see below). They often make predictions with nonlinearities that are difficult or impossible to encode explicitly.

For example, the relationship between income and health may not be linear; however, it can nonetheless be predicted by a regression model trained on data containing both variables.

No nonlinearity: Models with no activation function or nonlinearity are called linear classifiers. Because they only use linear combinations of features in their prediction step. Linear classifiers usually have less accuracy than more complex models but require fewer parameters to train and operate.

Configuration 2: Sigmoid – Prediction of Probabilities with No Relationship

Sigmoid activation functions are used for binary classification problems. In other words, they are used to determine whether an input belongs to a class or not. The sigmoid function takes in a number between 0 and 1 and outputs a value within the same range. The output of this function is always either 0 or 1, where 0 means false and 1 means true.

Configuration 3: SoftMax – Prediction of Which-One Probabilities

In the SoftMax function, you give a vector of scores to a neuron, which returns a probability distribution over the classes. So, for example, if you were predicting which-one probabilities (i.e., predicting which category is more likely). Then your input would be the output of a previous layer in the network, and your output would be the probability that class A was chosen over class B:

- The SoftMax function takes an array of scores and returns an array of probabilities for each possible outcome. For example, it might return this output: [0.2, 0.9, 0.8], which means that there is only a 20% chance that Class A is correct, a 90% chance that Class B is correct, and an 80% chance that Class C is right.

- The SoftMax function is used to predict the probability of each class. For example, if you have a set of classes called A, B, and C, SoftMax might give us that A is 0.2% likely, B is 90% likely, and C is 8% likely.

Inputs Are Similar

When building a neural network, you'll typically have training data provided to the model in the form of inputs and corresponding outputs. Inputs can be very similar; for example, in a classification task, it's not uncommon for the output classes to be completely different (e.g., dog vs. cat) but for the input features to be quite similar (e.g., the shape of ears).

This type of "similarity" between inputs is problematic because it makes it difficult for the network to generalize well. Even if you train your model on 100 samples, there are clear distinctions between each pair of classes. Suppose those pairs are extremely similar (e.g., one has a small black patch on its ear). Then your final model will likely perform poorly when tested against novel examples from other categories with different characteristics but which rely on similar features (for example, brown patches instead of black ones).

Activation functions are used to transform the input into a form that is more suitable for the neural network. They perform this transformation by squiggling or turning the input to match the activation function's requirements. For example, your inputs should also be within those bounds if you have an activation function with values between 0 and 1.

SoftMax Computation

In machine learning, the function that maps an array of real-valued vectors to a probability distribution over the same vectors is called the SoftMax function. The SoftMax function is used in the context of logistic regression and multinomial logistic regression.

In contrast, other functions used for probabilistic modeling, such as cross-entropy and log loss, are invertible (i.e., they can be used both forward and backward). There is no inverse operation associated with the SoftMax operator. Thus, we have learned to think about this conceptually: applying our model to some data gives us some output (which may be categorical or continuous). It doesn't matter if you call this result' probabilities' or 'memberships.' Still, it should be consistent across all memberships/probabilities under consideration for your final predictive results not to contradict themselves!

How to Install Activation Instructions

Activation functions are implemented as Python class constructors or factory methods. They have one required argument: a list of layers to which they will be applied (the input), along with any additional arguments that certain types may require of activation functions (if applicable). Activation functions create an output layer by applying their activation function to all previous layers specified in their constructor parameter list. This means that you must specify a loss layer if you want to use an activation function on top of a loss layer; if not specified explicitly, no output layer will be applied by default!

In a mathematical sense, the activation function's slope is the output's derivative. Put another way, it's the change in output for a change in input.

So why not just multiply delta by the input? The answer lies in how we interpret our learning rate (LR). If you multiply your learning rate by 1 and pass it through an activation function with a slope of 1, then this would be equivalent to multiplying its original value by 100%. This would allow you to learn much faster than you really should! It's important to keep your learning rates small so that they don't influence how quickly your model learns from training data.

As you can see, there is a linear relationship between the output of a neuron and the input. We call this slope the derivative, which is another name for slope. The derivative is simply a function of the input and weights of a neuron.

For example, let's say we have two neurons that each takes as inputs numbers 0 to 1 and then multiply by some weights (0 to 1). If we connect these two neurons in series with one another and give them an input value k = 0.5, then their outputs will be:

```
Derivative1 = 1 x 0 + -1 x 1 = 3/2 (because
-1 x 1 = -1)

Derivative2 = 0 x 0 + 2 x 1 + 4 x 2 = 6
(because 2x1+4x2=6)
```

So, we can see that the derivative of a neuron is just a function of its input and weights. You may be wondering how this can be useful.

Chapter 9

Introducing Convolutional
Neural Networks

Convolutional Neural Networks, or CNNs, are multi-layer neural networks popularized by Yann LeCun and his team in the late 1990s. They were originally designed to classify images, such as identifying whether an image contained a car or not. However, they're used for almost everything imaginable, including object detection and segmentation in images, natural language processing (NLP), speech recognition, and synthesis. Moreover, these networks don't just work well with highly constrained tasks like classification: they can also handle sequences (like audio) and time series data (like stock market prices). In other words, they have proved themselves useful for general-purpose AI applications!

Convolutional Neural Networks

Neural networks are powerful tools for learning about your data. But what if you want to use them for more than just classification? What if you want to use a neural network to learn about some property of your data and then use this learned property in a new prediction? In this chapter, we'll look at an example: using convolutional neural networks (CNNs) to learn about edges and corners in images.

CNNs are often used for image processing because they're very good at detecting patterns of lines or edges in images. For example, imagine that you're looking at an image of a tiger—you might be able to tell right away that something is interesting going on over its shoulder because it seems like there must be another animal there! But how would we go about actually finding out what's happening behind the tiger? We could start by looking at all possible ways the lines could have been drawn together (or "connected"). Then, if those lines happen to form something that looks like an animal head or body part—well, hey presto! We've found something interesting! You see where I'm going with this: CNNs can detect objects even if they don't appear explicitly in an image; instead, they figure out whether certain guesses made sense based on what other regions were nearby.

Reusing Weights in Multiple Places

In practice, the idea of reusing weights can be a bit confusing. There are two main ways that this happens:

Weights can be shared across different layers. For example, a layer might use the same weights for every position (a filter). Or it might use the same weights for every image in a batch, which could mean using different filters at each position on an image.

Weights may also be shared across different channels of one or more images in a batch—this is called channel-wise convolutional neural networks and is used when dealing with color images (like photos). For instance, you could have three different channels: red, green, and blue (RGB), where each channel is represented by its own set of filters; or you could instead think about each pixel having three values representing its intensity for red, green blue components.

Why are they called 'convolutional'?

The name "convolutional" comes from an operation in linear algebra called convolution. Convolution is used to process images, audio, and text, but it can also be used for other data types such as time series.

Convolution is an inner product between two functions (see Figure 2-1). In the case of images, each function has dimensions: width x height x channels (red, green, blue).

Convolutional layers are small, linear layers. It's called "convolution" because it's the same as multiplying two matrices. There are a lot of convolutional layers in each position in an image, so many features can be extracted from one image.

In CNNs, convolutional layers make up most of the network structure and can be used for feature extraction (pixels in an image). In this way, CNNs are very efficient at extracting high-level features from data without explicitly modeling the low-level details of those images (e.g., edges).

Basic Kernel Operation

A convolutional layer consists of a 2D filter that slides over the input image and outputs a single number. The output value is calculated by summing up all values along the filter's "scanning path" over the input image. The result is called an activation map, which can be viewed as a positive or negative number depending on whether it is higher or lower than some threshold value.

The term "activation map" may sound vague. Still, there's nothing mysterious about it: It just means we're combining (or activating) the pixels in our convolutional layer into one value (the activation map). Once we've got that activation map, we use its values to decide how to change our network's weights for future training steps.

Kernels as Feature Detectors

When you first hear about convolutional neural networks, it's important to understand that each kernel is essentially a small linear filter that detects features in the image. The kernels are applied to each pixel in the image and detect features. In this case, we're applying a 3x3 filter (a 3x3 grid of numbers) to every pixel in our input image. This gives us an output matrix with 1s at all points, edges or corners, and zeros everywhere else.

Padding, Stride, and Kernel Size

It is important to know that padding, stride, and kernel size are all parameters of the CNN. Padding is the amount of space added to the right and bottom of an image. Stride is the number of pixels between the center of one kernel and the center of the next kernel. Finally, kernel size is the number of pixels in each direction a given filter spans when applied over different parts of your image.

Pooling Layers

Pooling layers reduce the dimensionality of inputs, which means that we have fewer parameters and connections in our network.

This is important because it allows us to train more efficiently and with more computational power.

Pooling can be done in two ways: max pooling and average pooling. Max pooling picks the maximum value from each feature map (the last hidden layer). Average pooling calculates an average value over all feature maps.

Max poolers are often used at earlier stages of a CNN. In contrast, average poolers make sense at later stages of training as they provide information about local regions while retaining some global context.

Convolutional Networks for Image Processing

Convolutional neural networks (CNNs) are the network of choice for image processing. They have been used in many domains such as image classification, object detection and segmentation, and recognition.

Although many different aspects make CNN great at performing these tasks, one of their biggest advantages is that they can learn features directly from an unlabeled dataset without requiring any external information about what the features mean or how they should be modeled. This allows them to automatically detect features that would otherwise be difficult or impossible for a human programmer to discover independently.

The idea behind convolutional neural nets is that they can learn by example and use their knowledge to classify new images. This is powerful because computers can now spot faces in pictures or recognize objects in real-world scenes (like recognizing a banana).

Neural Networks That Understand Language

It's difficult to imagine the impact a machine that could understand language would have on our world. The idea is so powerful yet simple; we think of them as "computers," but what if they could feel like us? What if they could truly understand their environment? We'll review some basics of Natural Language Processing (NLP), then dive into how to use these techniques to build your NLP models. To get started, let's take a look at why this is important in the first place:

Natural Language Processing (NLP)

Natural language processing (NLP) is the field of study devoted to creating computational systems that can understand and produce natural language text. NLP is a subfield of artificial intelligence and machine learning, which means it's used in many applications such as search engines, spell checkers, and machine translation.

Neural networks are helpful for NLP because they can learn to recognize patterns in a large amount of data without being explicitly programmed to do so. For example, let's say you're trying to build a neural network to recognize if someone is talking about "stop signs" or "red lights." Training this neural network on historical data from previous examples of stop signs or red lights will teach how those different words are related based on their context within sentences. After this training process has been

141

completed successfully, repeatedly repeated until accuracy reaches desired levels (i.e., when our model correctly answers 80%+ times). We then apply what we've learned in new situations where we haven't seen any training data yet - like when someone mentions stopping signs while driving down the highway at night!

Supervised NLP

Supervised NLP works by training neural networks on large text datasets and the corresponding labels for each piece of text. This allows the neural network to learn what words mean, how they relate to other words in a sentence, and how those relationships change from one phase to another.

The benefit is that these methods can be used to train an AI system with knowledge about language, which helps it make predictions about whether new pieces of data have similar characteristics as previous ones.

One limitation is that, unlike other machine learning techniques (such as unsupervised NLP), supervised NLP requires enormous datasets with labeled examples for the system to function well. It also has trouble interpreting sentences where the subject occurs late in a sentence or where there are multiple subjects within one sentence. These are common problems when training a chatbot using supervised NLP because chatbots tend not to have full context available during conversations with users.

Applications include chatbots and speech recognition software like Amazon Alexa. However, you should keep in mind that this category refers primarily to recreational uses such as entertainment products; very few companies have successfully commercialized their products using supervised NLP due mainly to its limitations, outlined above!

Capturing Word Correlation in Input Data

One key to making a neural network that understands language is to capture the relationship between words. For example, imagine you're building a machine learning model that determines which kind of restaurant to recommend to users based on their previous orders. Rather than just using the number of times someone orders pizza to make recommendations, you could also look at other recently ordered foods. For example, if someone has ordered pizza and wings in the past, it makes sense for your model to consider recommending a wing joint and another pizza place.

This can be done using a correlation matrix (which maps out pairs of words and returns their similarity level). The following code describes how this would work:

```python
correlation_matrix = [correlate(row1[i],
row2[i]) for ii in range(len(row1))] #
iterate through rows

```

This would produce an array of values representing the correlation between different input words. The more similar two words are (meaning they appear together in sentences, articles, etc.), their corresponding value will be higher—and vice versa if they aren't very similar.

Predicting Movie Reviews

We will use a neural network to predict the sentiment of movie reviews. The neural network uses word embeddings to predict the sentiment score of each study and then uses supervised machine learning to classify each review as positive or negative.

We will use a pre-trained word embedding from Stanford University that was trained on the Google News dataset. This embedding assigns numerical values (0–1) to terms based on their context within a sentence. For example, if we have an input sentence that contains "I loved this movie," then our task is much easier because "loved" has a high value for sentiment, whereas "hated" has a low value for the sentiment. If, instead, we had an input sentence with "Hated it!" it becomes much harder because there are no recognizable words with high or low values respectively. However, by using all three words together, we can still make an educated guess about how the user felt about this particular movie based upon how similar those words were in other movies and what their overall average was across all movies (which would be around 0).

Introduction to an Embedding Layer

A word embedding layer maps words to vectors or points in space. Words with similar meanings will be closer together in the vector space than words with different meanings. For example, the words "dog" and "cat" are close together in a vector space because they both refer to animals we typically keep as pets. The same goes for the words "dog" and "horse."

Embeddings can also be used to predict similarity between two words by computing their cosine distance using trigonometry:

```
cos(A + B) = cos A * cos B - sin A * sin B
```

In this example, the word "cat" is close to "dog," which means it's likely similar. However, the word "horse" isn't as close to "cat." That says something about how people think of these animals: they're not the same, but they're still related in some way.

Interpreting the Output

You'll also see a similarity between word embeddings and neural networks. In the previous section, we saw how a neural network could take in a string of numbers (representing an image) and produce another set of numbers (representing an output). Likewise, in this section, we saw how the word embedding model could take in a word like "cat" and produce a vector containing the key features that make up that word.

This is powerful! But it gets even better because you can use these vectors to understand relationships between words or concepts without explicitly defining those relationships yourself.

Neural Architecture

Neural networks are machine learning models that can learn to perform tasks by observing examples and adjusting their internal parameters. The idea is that, given enough training data with feedback on the accuracy of their predictions, neural networks can find patterns in the data that humans may not have been able to discover just by looking at it. A neural network consists of layers (or "layers" for short) which you can think about as stacked neurons. Each layer has some neurons, and each has a set of parameters called weights and biases (more on these later).

When you train a neural network, you give it input data X along with labels Y=1 or Y=0 depending on whether your output should be 1 or 0, respectively. Then, using backpropagation, you adjust the weights and biases so that your model's predictions match your labels as closely as possible. This process is repeated until no further improvement is observed in its accuracy — this happens when we have reached an equilibrium where our loss function converges because we have overfitted our model to the training data.

Comparing Word Embeddings

Let's look at how word embeddings can be used to compare words.

First, let's create a new neural network. We'll use the same architecture as before but with a smaller batch size (10) and fewer epochs (100).

```r
```{r setup}

library(tidytext)

library(wordcloud)

data(corpus_train_body_clean)

corpus % anti_join(stop_words) %>%
filter(!is.na(word)) %>% unnest() %>%
mutate(word = strsplit(word, " ")) %>%
arrange(-ngram_size) -> trainCorpus

neural net(trainCorpus$word ~
trainCorpus$context) -> model
```

Neural Networks Don't Learn Data, They Minimize The Loss Function.

So, what does it mean for your neural network to minimize a loss function? First, it means that the network is minimizing its error as it learns data.

147
```

The loss function is a function of both the parameters of the neural network and its inputs. This means that there are multiple ways to think about what kind of knowledge is being created by training a neural network:

The choice of loss function determines how much your neural net will know when you train it on data (i.e., if you choose the wrong loss function, then your model might not be able to generalize well)

How weights change through training also determines what kind of knowledge they create.

In other words, neural networks don't learn data; they minimize the loss function.

The Choice of Loss Function Determines the Neural Network's Knowledge

The loss function is what the neural network learns. It's what we want to minimize, which means it's an excellent place to start when building a neural network that understands the language.

The loss function measures how well our neural network predicts the correct output for each word in the sentence above (we'll call this task "word prediction"). The loss function compares these predictions to what is actually in the sentence and calculates a difference between them. For example, if our word prediction was "dog" and there only exist three words in the sentence ("cat," "dog," and "eat"), then our predicted value would be incorrect by two units (sorry, doggies). This error can be measured as $1 - 0 = 1$

in this case; larger values represent worse performance because they indicate more mistakes made by your model during training time.

Larger values also indicate that your model has learned less about how these relationships work — i.e., if you have no idea how cats relate to dogs, then it should take longer than if you already know something about them beforehand!

Word Analogies

Word analogies are a way to measure how well a neural network understands the relationships between words. This is an essential skill since it enables a computer to understand the intended meaning of sentences like "the dog bit the bone" and "the bone was bitten by the dog."

The word analogy problem can be framed as follows: given two input words, A and B, find another word C that has a similar meaning or relationship to A and B. So, for example, for input pairs (apple-pear), (dog-cat), and (pencil-pen), we want our model to produce answers like fruit, mammal, and writing utensil as correct answers for each pair.

So, in summary, neural networks that understand language are a complex but exciting field. They're still in their infancy, and there's a lot more to be done before they can be deployed on a wide scale, but the potential of this technology is huge. We look forward to seeing how it develops over time!

Chapter 10

Recurrent Layers
for Variable-Length Data

A recurrent neural network is a particular kind of neural network that can learn to model data sequences using an internal state. They're often used to generate sequences, like writing text or creating music. These networks are also called "recurrent" because they have loops: information flows through the loops repeatedly as the computer writes it down.

The RNN

Recurrent neural networks are neural networks used for sequence prediction tasks. They can be trained too long model sequences; thus, they are also called "long short-term memory" (LSTM) networks. The hidden state of an RNN at time step t refers to the state of the network at time step t after considering all previous inputs. This means it contains information about all previous outputs from the model and all input up until time step t. In other words, you can think of the hidden state as a "memory" for your model.

In general, there are many types of recurrent layers and their specific implementations depending on what task you're trying to solve: whether it involves modeling temporal relationships between events or any type of sequence prediction task (such as language modeling).

Backpropagation through Time

To train a neural network, we need an error function. The error is the difference between the predicted target value (or input) and the actual target value (or input). Here's what we do:

First, we evaluate all of our training examples using our neural network.

Next, we calculate the predicted outputs using backpropagation through time.

Then, we compare these predicted outputs with the actual outputs of our training examples. We then use this comparison to determine how much each weight should be changed to improve previous results. This is called gradient descent on a cost function.

Vanishing and Exploding Gradients

One of the main reasons why recurrent layers fail to work is that they have a problem called vanishing and exploding gradients.

Explaining this problem is simple: if you have only a few examples, then it's easy for all your weights to be close to zero or one (or some other extreme value) and thus not learn anything. This is known as vanishing gradients because most of the weights will be near zero, thus not learning anything new. On the other hand, if you have too many examples, then all your weights may end up being very large values that don't change much during training time and thus can't generalize well either! This phenomenon is called exploding gradients because there are so many possible large values for each weight that it becomes impossible for them all to converge into reasonable values during training.

LSTMs (Long-Short Term Memory)

This section will explore the LSTM (long-short term memory) architecture. LSTMs are a type of recurrent neural network that is capable of learning long-term dependencies.

LSTMs are also known as memory cells because they use internal memory to model sequences with variable lengths. This is an important distinction because it means you can train your LSTM model on huge data sets without worrying about the input data size and its corresponding time complexity. In other words, an LSTM model doesn't require any preprocessing before training it!

GRUs (Gated Recurrent Units)

You can use an RNN to model sequences of discrete events. But the process is often more complicated than it needs to be. GRUs are a type of recurrent layer designed to deal with this problem by being simpler to implement, train and use than LSTMs and other models.

GRU stands for "Gated Recurrent Unit," just like LSTM does. However, their unique architecture helps them learn sequences better than vanilla RNNs (no gating units).

The difference between the two architectures is that LSTM has more gating units that control when information passes in or out of each cell (or memory cell) in the network. In contrast, GRUs only have one type of gating unit which controls access during an input sequence - there's no backpropagation through the time required for long-term information storage as you get with LSTMs!

Implementation with TensorFlow

You must first import the necessary modules to implement recurrent layers in TensorFlow. These include:

- TensorFlow as tf

- NumPy as np

- math

- os (OS-specific functions)

- sys (system-level calls)

- time (time-related functions)

- random (random values)

A Tutorial with Code on Implementing Recurrent Neural Layers for Variable Length Data with TensorFlow

A recurrent neural layer is a neural network that can be trained to process variable length datasets. It works by having a sequence of inputs that processes one element at a time and then outputs the same sequence after processing. This allows it to work on data with variable lengths, such as text or audio recordings, where some elements in the data may be longer than others (e.g., sentences).

Recurrent layers are also known as "long short-term memory" (LSTM) layers because they use LSTM units for their processing units and gates. Again, we will use TensorFlow for our code examples but feel free to try training these networks using Keras instead if you have experience with Keras!

The TensorFlow documentation has a lot of information about recurrent layers and how to use them. They also have some example code on GitHub, but it is not very easy to understand, so this tutorial will give you more details about what each step does.

1. Import the TensorFlow module, and create a graph object with tf.Graph(), and then create a session object with

tf.Session() . We also need to initialize all variables before using them by calling tf.global_variables_initializer(). Then we can run our code inside of this session to get results.

2. Create placeholders for our data and define the shape and type of each placeholder. The first placeholder is for the input data and has an unknown number of rows and 20 columns because we don't know how many objects are in our dataset yet. The second placeholder is for the targets, which also have an unknown number of rows but only 1 column because each target represents just one class label.

3. We can now build the model by defining a function that will create a cell and then run it over multiple time steps using tf.nn.dynamic_rnn(). This function takes in the cell, the input data, and its length (num_steps) as inputs and then outputs a sequence of states for each step (states), as well as an output value at the last step (output). We must define this cell before creating it with tf.nn.

4. Once the model is created, we can train it by creating a tf.train.AdamOptimizer() calls the minimize function on it with our loss function as an argument. It will then apply gradients to update the weights and biases. We also need to define another placeholder that will hold our learning rate so we can modify it later if we want to play around with different values.

5. Finally, we need a way to evaluate the model's performance. We will add a placeholder (labels) that holds our true class labels and then compare them with the predictions from the model. We get these values by computing tf.nn.softmax() on the output and then comparing it with our true labels with tf.argmax(prediction, 1). This gives us a tensor of dimension batch_size x 1 where each value is either 0 or 1 depending on whether we correctly predicted the class.

Code the RNN Layer for variable length data

First, we need to import the necessary libraries. We'll use the TensorFlow library for creating our RNN layer and then add it to our graph. After that, we can create the variables for our inputs, outputs and initial state of our RNN layer.

Then we need to set our input tensors (glimpse at column 0), output tensors (destination) and initial state tensor (first element in your source).

And finally set your RNN layer output size.

```
import tensorflow as tf #create a RNN Cell
layer called rnn_cell rnn_cell =
tf.contrib.rnn.BasicRNNCell(num_units=128)
#attach the RNN cell layer to our graph by
calling the rnn function outputs, state =
tflearn.flatten(tflearn.layers.recurrent({'r
nn': rnn_cell}, inputs)) #variables

inputs = tf.placeholder(tf.float32,
shape=(None, None, 1)) # input tensor
```

```
outputs = tf.placeholder(tf.float32,
shape=(None, 1)) # output tensor
initial_state = tf.placeholder(tf.float32,
shape=(None, 128)) # RNN Cell's initial
state

#attributes of the RNN cell
rnn_cell.set_inputs(tflearn.layers.flatten(i
nputs)) # set input tensors
rnn_cell.set_outputs(outputs) # set output
tensors rnn_cell.set_state(initial_state) #
set initial state rnn_cell.set_nodes(128) #
set number of nodes in the RNN layer
```

Chapter 11

Introducing
Automatic Optimization

D eep learning is an incredibly powerful tool for building machine intelligence. It's also accessible: most deep learning frameworks are open source and free to use. As a result, they can be applied to problems as diverse as image recognition and natural language processing (NLP). However, there's no such thing as a free lunch—every framework has its strengths and weaknesses. For example, if your goal is providing maximum performance at all costs, you might need to deal with some tradeoffs regarding ease of use or flexibility. If this sounds familiar, don't worry: we've got just what you need!

Differentiating a Basic Neural Network

A feedforward neural network is a type of artificial neural network that takes a set of input values and produces a set of output values. As the name suggests, there is no feedback between the layers, so any change to an input value only results in changes in its corresponding output value.

What Is a Deep Learning Framework?

A deep learning framework is a collection of tools that make it easier to build deep learning models. In other words, it's an application programming interface (API) for building computer vision applications. These APIs are built on top of other frameworks, so each layer represents another level in the stack. This architecture allows you to focus on specific tasks while letting the low-level parts care for themselves. You can think of this as similar to how you might use an OS like Windows or Mac OSX;

159

they have many built-in features that allow you to do basic things like copy files from one folder to another without having to write code yourself — just click and drag!

Good Tools Reduce Errors, Speed Development, and Increase Runtime Performance

The process of building deep learning frameworks is hard, but not for the reasons you might think. Instead, the difficulty has more to do with time than intellect: it takes a long time to build a framework from scratch. To help reduce the amount of time required to build and optimize these advanced machine learning systems, we've created an open-source library called Automatic Differentiation (AD). AD is an extension of TensorFlow that allows you to use automated differentiation techniques like backpropagation and stochastic gradient descent in your models without writing any code! That's right; no more hand-written gradients or partial derivatives - just define your model once and let AD handle all the heavy lifting.

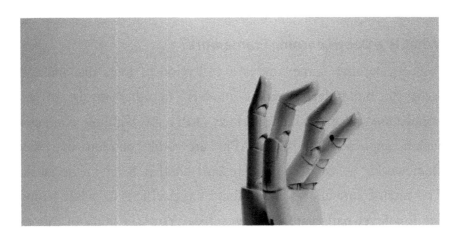

Using AD will save you countless hours each week and make it easier for others on your team to contribute their improvements without fear of introducing bugs or performance issues into existing code bases (thus breaking everything). Best yet? It can be used alongside frameworks like Keras so that when someone says, "let me try this cool new technique," there won't be any hesitation since switching between different libraries won't require rewriting everything again either!

Forward and Back Propagation

Forward propagation is the process of taking an input and computing a prediction. In our example, we pass in a 5-by-5 image and use it to predict the class (cat or dog). This can be done by applying convolutional layers to the image and using an activation function such as ReLU or SoftMax.

Forward propagation has two parts: computation and backpropagation. The former involves running your model on your data, while backpropagation refers to how you optimize this process so that it's always getting better at modeling your data. In practice, we usually combine these steps into one forward propagation step on our training set with each iteration of our training loop—which makes sense since they both rely on having access to predictions from previous iterations!

Automated Differentiation

Automatic differentiation (AD) is a technique that allows you to compute the derivative of an arbitrary function. For example, suppose you have the function "f" defined over a set of inputs "x" and outputs "y":

```python
def f(x):

... # implementation goes here.
```

The AD framework will take this function definition as input and return its gradient concerning each parameter, which can be used for optimization. Furthermore, because the framework handles all of the differentiation computations, it's possible to write deep learning models that don't require manually computing gradients for every layer separately — saving a lot of time!

Automatic Optimization for Deep Learning Frameworks

Automatic optimization is a way to find the best parameters for a neural network automatically. For example, if you want to train a neural network with 100 neurons in each layer and 3 hidden layers, what should be the size of each neuron? Should they all have the same size, or should they be different? What is the best learning rate to use? These are all questions that can be answered by automatic optimization.

Automatic optimization generates random parameter sets and then tries them out on your dataset. If it finds any improvement, then it will update its results accordingly (hopefully). It does this repeatedly until it reaches an acceptable error level (or another metric).

Tensors are a generalization of vectors and matrices. They're higher-dimensional generalizations of them. A tensor is what you get when you have multiple dimensions that aren't arranged in columns or rows—they're mixed up together, making it impossible to represent them as one-dimensional objects like vectors or matrices.

A good way to think about how those two types of tensors differ is by considering how we would represent them visually. For example, say we want to show the relationship between height and weight on a scatterplot (a graph where each point represents one person). We could label this graph with height and weight dimensions instead of just one dimension because they're related. Still, if we were only labeling people according to their weights, there wouldn't be enough room on our plot—we'd have no way of making space for all potential combinations! So instead, we'd use two different plots: one for height vs. weight (with points representing individuals) and another for height vs. age (with points representing groups).

Introducing Autograd - Automatic Gradient Computation

The Automatic Gradient Computation is a library that automatically computes derivatives as you go, making your code much more concise. It's used in many deep learning frameworks, including TensorFlow and PyTorch.

This is an important concept to understand because it allows us to write our neural network code with little effort on the programmer's part.

You've seen that the problem of calculating gradients for a neural network can get quite involved. Thankfully, there is a way to automate this process through automatic differentiation. The autograd package provides automatic differentiation, allowing us to quickly calculate gradients with little effort.

Tensor is a generalization of matrices and vectors, so it can be thought of as a matrix with more than one column or row. The elements in the tensor are called nodes, which are arranged in some order. Each node has an associated index: 0, 1, 2...

The tensor provides a very basic framework for storing elements in any number of dimensions. However, the most important thing about using the tensor is that it makes it easy to manipulate your data.

This operation is equivalent to multiplying a two-dimensional matrix with the same number of rows and columns as the original tensor. The result is that the new element at index i, j will be

We'll first build a function that takes a tensor and returns the same tensor with some modifications. It will use the variable name "a" to make it easy to understand what we are doing.

```python
def modify(tensor, value):
```

We want this to be a one-time operation, so we ensure that `tensor` is used only once in this function.

```python
if (len(tensor) != 1):

raise ValueError("Tensor must consist of a single element")
```

Now, let's look at how the compiler would optimize this function. It will replace `tensor` with `value` and remove the part that checks if the element count of a tensor is 1. This optimization process will reduce our code size by a lot!

What is a tensor? A tensor is simply a way of representing multiuse data. Let's look at some examples.

In the first example, you have two separate tensors that are used multiple times by your model:

```
(X_1, X_2) = [0.5, 0],

(Y_1, Y_2) = [1].
```

In the second example, there is only one instance of a single tensor that is used for both input and output signals:

```
(X_{input}, X_{output}) = [0.5].
```

How Addition Backpropagation Works

Backpropagation is a method to compute the gradient of a loss function concerning a set of parameters. It's an algorithm that allows you to improve your model's performance by learning from data and updating weights accordingly.

But it turns out that there is more than one way to do this, and which method you use will have an impact on how fast your model learns and whether you can generalize well or not.

Negation Support

Now that you've learned how to define and use layers let's add support for Negation. While it might seem like adding this one layer type would be easy, consider the case where we want to negate a vector whose dimension is n (where n is not a power of two). To do this with our current neural network framework, we would have to write code that looks something like this:

```
def __neg__(self, other): x =
self.expand(other) y = -1 * x return y
```

Now let's say we want to add support for additional functions like sin, cos, and tan. To do this with our current neural network framework, we would have to write code that looks something like this:

```
def sin(self, x): return self.tanh(x) def
cos(self, x): return self.cosh(x) def
tan(self, x): return self.tanh_complex(x
```

While this code will work, it's not very elegant. It's quite ugly. Fortunately, there is a better way to write this code. And that is the Neural network framework.

One way to support Negation and other functions is by adding layers containing layers. For example, let's say we want to add a layer called Negation which contains another layer. We could write this code:

```
class Negation(Layer): def __init__(self,
child): self.child = child def forward(self,
x): return -1 * self.child.forward(x) def
backward(
```

Additional Function Support

Now that we have autograd and the symbolic differentiation framework, let's add support for additional functions. This will enable us to optimize our neural networks more effectively. In particular, we'll need support for addition, subtraction, multiplication, and division. Support for these functions is readily

167

available in NumPy or SciPy, so it's not hard to implement them in PyTorch.

The only thing left is figuring out how they should be used during backpropagation through time (BPTT). It turns out that addition and multiplication are used sparingly during BPTT because their corresponding gradients usually replace them. This works well because when computing the gradient of a function at a specific x value using a forward pass through your neural network (this involves feeding inputs into a matrix of weights). You can also perform forward passes with different values of w until you find one where $f(x) = 0$.

Once this happens—and assuming there aren't any other equalities involving $f(x)$ —we know that adding or multiplying terms together won't change the result since those terms won't exist anymore!

```
So if we wanted to compute gradients w_2 =
w_1 - h(z_2), where h(z) = tanh((z)) ,
```

then our expression becomes:

```
dW/dz = dW/dx + (1/2)*dW/(dx*dx) which drops
out as soon as we divide both sides by dx!
```

Training Neural Networks with Autograd

While training is an important part of building a neural network, it's easy to forget that we still need to test our results and ensure they meet expectations. We also have to scale the number of variables being fed into the model, which can be difficult without changing your code every time. Finally, debugging will become increasingly important as your neural network grows in complexity, so learning to debug before you get stuck in a situation with no way out is crucial. These are some of the reasons why having Autograd available helps developers create deep learning frameworks— because it allows them access to all these benefits:

- Test-driven development (TDD)

- Scalability

- Simplicity

Automatic Optimization

Automatic optimization is a feature that allows you to automatically adjust the weights of your neural network while it's being trained. This means you can use automatic optimization to find the optimal configuration for your model without manually tuning all its parameters, saving you time and improving your results.

While using an automatic optimizer may sound like an easy way around tuning, there are some caveats: firstly, it's important to know how the optimizer works so that you can interpret its results correctly; secondly, there's still a lot of manual work involved in making sure that your model is correctly configured before training with automatic optimization enabled; finally (and most importantly), it's not always possible for an automatic optimizer to find better performance than what can be achieved by hand-tuned models.

To add an optimizer:

Click "Optimization" in the left navigation pane under "Deep Learning."

Select "Automatic Optimization" from this menu and click "Add New Model" under "Optimized Models" at the bottom right corner of the page

Support for Layer Types

Let's add support for layer types. This will allow us to build a deep learning framework that can perform automatic optimization.

We'll start with loss-function layers, which are used in the following operations:

- Cross entropy loss

- SoftMax cross-entropy loss

- Log SoftMax cross-entropy loss

Similarly, we need nonlinearity layers for:

- Rectified Linear Units (ReLU) activation function

- Sigmoid activation function

- Tanh activation function * Leaky ReLU activation functions

Layers with Layers

You might wonder, "Why do we need layers that contain layers?"

The answer is simple: we can make our models more expressive with less code. That's right — less code! Imagine if you had to write out every single layer individually in your neural network model. You'd have hundreds of lines of code just to define a basic neural net structure (plus whatever else you add on top). Instead, with this new construct, all those layers are already defined for you in the building blocks of AutoML Vision's base architecture layer.

This isn't just about saving time, though—it also allows us to represent more complex machine learning concepts like CNNs and RNNs more succinctly than ever before. For example, let's say we want to build a convolutional neural network capable of classifying images into one-of-50 categories from the ImageNet dataset using ResNet50 as our base architecture layer — all we would need is four lines:

```python

network =
AutoMLVision(base_architecture="resnet50")

network =
AutoMLVision(base_architecture="resnet50")

layer =
AutoMLVision(base_architecture="resnet50").g
et_layer("conv") model =
Model(inputs=network.input, outputs=layer)
```

As you can see, using AutoML Vision's base architecture layers makes it much easier to build complex machine learning architectures like ResNet50 or VGG19 that were previously only possible with custom code. It's also faster than ever because these networks are already trained on hundreds of thousands of images—we just need the right parameters (like layer weights) and input data (to update those weights).

Loss-Function Layers

Loss-function layers determine whether or not the neural network is performing well. In other words, they use a loss function to tell us if our model is working as intended. Typically, this involves calculating how far away our predictions are from actual values and using that distance to determine how well our model is performing.

Learning Frameworks

There are a few ways to learn a framework. First, you can start with the syntax. This is important because it's the first thing every developer must learn to use the framework. Then, once you are familiar with what things look like and how they work together, you can learn about the functionality and how it works inside your favorite framework.

After that, it becomes more about using your favorite tools in real scenarios (or ones that interest you). You will probably want to customize your code along the way — making sure it does exactly what you need or want it to do — so this phase involves both writing code for yourself and being able to contribute back once complete!

Nonlinearity Layers

The deep learning frameworks we've seen are called feedforward neural networks because they have a single forward pass through the layers. In contrast, recurrent neural networks have cycles in their graph and can process data sequences.

They also require several additional components to be added to the framework:

A stateful component keeps track of what has been processed so far; this is typically an array or dictionary but could be stored as an attribute on each layer (this approach is recommended when using Keras).

An update function that takes an input sequence containing multiple timesteps and returns an output prediction for each timestep. To use this function, you must specify how many timesteps should be used in your model's inputs (you can do this by setting input_shape on your RNN layer).

The Embedding Layer

The Embedding layer is used to map from one space to another. It converts categorical data into continuous data and can be used to convert unlabeled data into labeled data.

Indexing and Autograd

The first thing we need to do is add indexing support for Autograd. This is a way to access a specific value in a tensor, basically just an n-dimensional array (where n is the number of dimensions). An example might be if you had the following matrix:

```
A = [[1, 2], [3, 4]]
```

Then you could find its third element using the expression A[2] (the indexing operator). This would return 3.

Another example would be if you had an array of lists:

```
B = [[1], [2], [3]]
```

Then you could get its third element using B[2]. Since lists are one-dimensional arrays, they only have one dimension, so there is no need for brackets around them when accessing elements like the above.

Cross-Entropy

The cross-entropy layer is a loss function layer, which simply means it's used to compute the loss function.

The loss function is the difference between predicted and actual values. It's essentially like a scorecard for your model: how well did you do? If your score is higher than zero, then you're doing okay! If not… well, there may be room for improvement in your model.

A common way of thinking about this is as follows: imagine that we have made predictions on a set of training data (a batch) and want to know how much those predictions differed from what occurred in reality (the ground truth). As such, we can use our trained neural network as an estimator for comparing those two numbers against each other using distance measures such as Euclidean or Hamming distance (more on these shortly).

Recurrent Neural Network

The Recurrent Neural Network Layer is a special layer that allows you to train your model to predict the future. This layer will be used in our deep learning framework to train a model based on input data and then use this trained model as an input for another prediction.

Using Automatic Differentiation to Build a Deep Learning Framework Is the Best Way to Build the Performance You Want

Automatic differentiation is a tool that allows you to build a deep learning framework without having to write any code.

We showed how upgrading Autograd to support multiuse tensors and adding support for multiple layers of the same type will help you build the performance you want. Then we used these new features to add indexing and loss-function layers with minimal effort on your part. In the end, we added automatic optimization capabilities so that as your models improve over time, they can automatically adapt themselves without any extra work from you!

Conclusion

In conclusion, we've learned that algorithms can be split into two main categories: deep learning and machine learning. Deep learning is a subset of machine learning, which is a subset of artificial intelligence.

The best way to grok an algorithm is to look at how it works and how it's used in practice.

The future of AI is here, and it's already changing lives.

As we've seen, machine learning has the power to make our lives easier, but it also has the potential to make them better. We can't wait to see what comes next!

Thank you for buying and reading/listening to our book. If you found this book useful/helpful please take a few minutes and leave a review on Amazon.com or Audible.com (if you bought the audio version).

References

Bachman, P. and Precup, D. (2015). Variational generative stochastic networks withcollaborative shaping. In Proceedings of the 32nd International Conference on Machine Learning, ICML 2015, Lille, France, 6-11 July 2015 , pages 1964–1972.

Alain, G., Bengio, Y., Yao, L., Éric Thibodeau-Laufer, Yosinski, J., and Vincent, P. (2015). GSNs: Generative stochastic networks. arXiv:1503.05571.

Bacon, P.-L., Bengio, E., Pineau, J., and Precup, D. (2015). Conditional computation in neural networks using a decision-theoretic approach. In 2nd Multidisciplinary Conference on Reinforcement Learning and Decision Making (RLDM 2015).

Ballard, D. H., Hinton, G. E., and Sejnowski, T. J. (1983). Parallel vision computation.

Nature

Cho, K., Raiko, T., and Ilin, A. (2011). Enhanced gradient and adaptive learning rate for training restricted Boltzmann machines. In ICML'2011 , pages 105–112.

Choromanska, A., Henaff, M., Mathieu, M., Arous, G. B., and LeCun, Y. (2014). The loss surface of multilayer networks.

Courbariaux, M., Bengio, Y., and David, J.-P. (2015). Low
precision arithmetic for deep learning. In Arxiv:1412.7024,
ICLR'2015 Workshop.

Fang, H., Gupta, S., Iandola, F., Srivastava, R., Deng, L., Dollár, P.,
Gao, J., He, X.,

Mitchell, M., Platt, J. C., Zitnick, C. L., and Zweig, G. (2015).
From captions to visual concepts and back.
arXiv:1411.4952.

www.ingramcontent.com/pod-product-compliance
Lightning Source LLC
Chambersburg PA
CBHW071153050326
40689CB00011B/2096